Why
Women
Weep

Why Women Weep

ALFREADA BROWN-KELLY

iUniverse, Inc.
Bloomington

WHY WOMEN WEEP

iUniverse books may be ordered through booksellers or by contacting:

iUniverse
1663 Liberty Drive
Bloomington, IN 47403
www.iuniverse.com
1-800-Authors (1-800-288-4677)

ISBN: 978-1-4620-2664-7 (sc)
ISBN: 978-1-4620-2663-0 (dj)
ISBN: 978-1-4620-2673-9 (ebk)

Printed in the United States of America

iUniverse rev. date: 06/01/2011

WHY WOMEN WEEP

Let's be real. Even Jesus wept. If I have learned anything in life, I have learned that we all have to cry sometimes. Some of us will cry more and some of us will cry less. Some of us will learn our lesson the first time, and some of us will have to repeat a chaotic episode four or five times. As females, we carry a heavy load. The weight of the world is on our shoulders. We are mothers, fathers, grandmothers, aunts, wives, doctors, lawyers, teachers, authors, business owners, administrative assistants, and we work in many other professions. We are expected to do and to keep doing. We cannot fall by the wayside because so many people are depending on us. We must not fail ourselves or others, but we are human.

As a result, sometimes life is going to make us sad and we will cry. But as women, who are expected to be everything to everybody, we must prevail. Even victory will not stop us from crying. Sometimes we will fall, but it is imperative that we get up again and again and again. We must teach our children, especially our girls, what is acceptable and appropriate behavior. We must insist that our girls treat other females the way they themselves want to be treated. We must consistently and constantly tell our girls that they will reap what they sow. If you sow bad seeds, you will reap a bad harvest. If you don't believe me, believe GOD. It is written in His Word.

All of the poetry in this book was created by me, except one poem, which was written by Patsy Bickerstaff. Some of the poems come from my two books, *Transformation of The Mind, Body & Soul* and *The Skin I Am In*. Many of the poems came to me as I began my journey writing this book.

Peace and blessings,
Alfreada Brown-Kelly

§

I had a colleague who was like a mother to me. I knew her for about nine years. She was one of my teachers in the nursing school and taught me how to teach. We loved each other; however, we would sometimes get into little disagreements just as mothers and daughters do. There was nothing I couldn't share with her, and her office was right across from mine. Sometimes, I would go sit and talk for a while when I was feeling stressed out about something or even when I was happy. Whatever she felt I needed to make my job easier, she would try to supply it for me. She was highly respected and a great grant writer for the school. Therefore, she had many connections. She sort of spoiled me, and we often ate and laughed together.

One Thursday evening after a long day of faculty meetings, someone came and told her that her car had a flat tire, so she called AAA or some other service company. Someone from the company came and fixed her tire, and then she began preparing to leave. She called me from her cell phone as she was leaving, asking me if I was okay. She said, "You seem a little stressed." I assured her I was okay and we said our good-byes. What I did not realize was this was a real GOOD-BYE.

That Sunday was "Founders Day" at the university, and I didn't hear from her and thought it was a little strange that she was not there. When I got home, I received the PHONE CALL. The person on the other end was another faculty member. She started the conversation by asking me if I was sitting down. My heart dropped and the only thing I heard her say was "Lydia, they found Mrs. _____." My daughter had to pick me up off the floor, and my mother finished the conversation on the phone.

I felt confused, depersonalized, abandoned, powerless, hopeless, and angry. I knew that Mrs. _____ didn't feel well some days, but I guess I just denied how badly she felt. Her daughter found her body at her home that Sunday after members missed her in church. We think she may have died Friday while attempting to go to work. I know she is in a better place and doesn't have to worry about the things we are still going through here, but I still cry sometimes when I think of her. I have a poem with her picture on it titled "When Tomorrow Starts Without Me." Reading the poem sometimes gives me comfort. My colleagues and the students were very supportive of me after her death. Although they loved her too, they knew how close we were to one another. Another teacher assisted me in teaching my class that semester. Mrs. _____'s daughter gave me so many of her personal items, and we remain friends today. I miss her so much and I'm crying now. However, I have grown stronger in my own right by remembering what she taught me, and I try to make her proud.

Dr. Lydia Figueroa

Dear _____

I know in my heart you had to go

But for those of you who have not been there

You couldn't possibly know

The burning pain in the center of my heart

Because you have departed

This place called Earth

Not to mention the disturbing thoughts

That has already begun to plague my mind

Because I can't pick up the phone

And talk to you all the time

My mentor, my friend, my superhero

A leader and mighty prayer warrior

You possessed a quiet and humble disposition

Always willing and ready to listen

Always willing to lend a helping hand

Like only my mentor could.

§

I weep because I am filled with joy knowing that God loves me. It took me a very long time to realize this, but now that I do, life is so simple. I used to put a lot of faith in man because I thought that was what I needed to do, but now I know better. Every day I am grateful that I asked Him to be in my life. Now, I fear nothing, except Him. Yes, at times, I may be worried, but when I am, I go to what I know that makes me whole. On some days, I don't talk to Him as often as I should, but I think He understands. After all, He made me and knows my every thought. Without Him, I am just another person caught in the world, but with Him, I am everything. But mostly, I am who He wants me to be: a faithful servant. I am not perfect and I never will be, but I am trying to be what it is He wants me to be. I find that when I go through Him for every move I make, life is a breeze. With Him, there is no uncertainty. I don't have to wonder. His will, will be done.

Another reason I weep is that I am sad that ignorance may never be overcome. People are quick to judge another by physical features and not by the person's character or content; it is a shame that we have to constantly prove ourselves to have people accept us. Why is that? We all look the same on the inside of our bodies. Yet, because a person's skin may be brown, red, or yellow, she or he is not given the same opportunities as others. Let us hope we move into a new era with our first Afro-American president. Then, we can learn from each other and not judge one another based on our skin color, but by our character and actions.

Debra Owens

WITH OR WITHOUT

Without Him
I cannot survive
With Him
I'll be able to thrive

Without Him
I am nothing
With Him
I am something

Without Him
I will bear much pain
With Him
I have everything to gain

Without Him
There is no hope
With Him
I'll be able to cope

Without Him
I'll live in fear
With Him
My mind is clear

Without Him
All hope is gone
With Him
I'll see Him on the throne.

§

Women weep for many reasons. A woman may weep when she feels like her man is receiving love but not giving out the love that she gives. A woman may weep when putting up with cheating, lying, and verbal abuse. A woman may weep when she has lowered her standards to please her man. A woman may weep when she tells her girlfriends, "Girl, I would leave my man if he did . . . ," but when he does, she still stays with him.

Weeping comes when a woman is not totally confident in herself. A confident woman does not have time to weep because the inner person is strong enough to choose the right man, a man who will not take her through the pain and drama that may cause her to weep. If every woman knew who God created her to be, the virtuous woman he spoke of in Proverbs, weeping would not be defined as cries of sadness but as Wisdom Enough to Encourage People. When you have the wisdom to encourage yourself, you will also have the power not to allow another human being to control your emotions.

Author Unknown

THET TELL US TO STAY STRONG

They tell us to stay strong

The pain will not last long

They tell us to pray

Because these doubts will go away

They tell us to forgive

So that we can be healed

They tell us life goes on

And

We will weather the storm

But let's be real

They don't know how we feel

From the hurt, disappointment, and pain

From the infidelities of a man.

§

These are the Best and Worst of Times

As women, there are many things that make us happy and just as many that make us sad. One of the happiest times in my life centered around the births of my two daughters. Once giving birth, I found that my heart was so filled with joy and thanks and a love that I had never before experienced. I was so thankful to our Lord, our God, for the blessed gifts he had given me, allowing me to experience the most fulfilling love, a love that had a depth that was not explainable in words. It was a love that allowed me to realize that their lives were more important than my own, and if the need ever arose, I would lay my life down and cease to exist if it meant that they could grow and prosper.

The saddest time of my life, unfortunately, was after the death of my grandmother, a woman who was full of life, strength, and love. She was a woman who was and still is a mentor to me. She was an example of what I have aspired to become, a good mother, a leader by example, and a nurturing individual. I remember the day of her death. I felt an overwhelming sense of loss and despair. I felt as though I had lost a part of myself, and a piece of my soul went with her to heaven and is still with her there today. I don't feel as though her death is a loss to my being; instead, I remain attached and connected to her, always remember her, and speak about her. My experience with this loss was a devastating time, but in time, I learned to talk to her and began to allow my grief to change me. I learned to celebrate her life and all of the wonderful contributions she made to me personally and to our family as a whole.

Dr. Melinda Barker

DO YOU KNOW THIS WOMAN?

A strong woman-with superhero powers

A humble woman-praying at every hour

A loving woman-respecting her man

A gentle woman-her children respect, love and understand

A tireless woman-making sure everything is okay

A grateful woman-thanking God for everything

A praying woman-giving thanks to the King

A faithful woman-discerning right from wrong

A holy woman-singing a praise song

Do you know this woman?

§

I am not a person who cries easily. I have never cried during a movie or a TV show. I did not even cry when my father died, although if I had, I would probably have recovered from the grief more quickly.

The incident that made me cry a lot was going into counseling to handle the depression I had as a result of my service as an Army nurse in Vietnam. It took a long time before the crying occurred. I returned from Vietnam in 1971 and did not cry until 1980. In 1980, I went to the Vet Center and joined a counseling group of all male combat veterans. When I first tried to explain what my service was like, I started to cry. I believed I cried for the next three weeks. I did not belong in that group. The men could not understand how I could be upset since I hadn't actually been in combat. My sorrow came from remembering the number of young, strong, healthy men I watched die. Even more so, I was affected by the fact that I could do nothing to make things better. I couldn't heal the guys, and I couldn't end the senseless war.

I learned that keeping problems bottled up inside does not make them fade; in fact, it makes them grow. After about three months with the group, I was referred to a psychotherapist. Again, it took a long time, but I finally reached a place where I could accept myself as not being a bad person because I could not help all of my patients. As I stated above, I do not cry easily, but I know enough to realize that even without tears I can release the sorrow by talking. I spent a long time talking to the counselor about my father's death. I didn't cry, but I did recover.

HE CAME INTO MY LIFE

I was torn, broken, and battered

He came into my life when it really mattered

I felt like dirt

Not to mention I was hurt

He spoke softly and firmly

Told me to hold my head up

I asked the question, "What for?"

"Why would you do me any favors?"

He said,

"Because I am the Great I Am—the God of a second chance"

"I am not sure that I understand"

He told me—He loved me unconditionally

"Why me?" I said

He held out His arms to me and said,

"Can't you see? You belong to me"

"My child, I will set you free."

§

We had been married for 18 years and I wanted a child very much. For years, there were many false alarms and tests that came out negative. It was heartbreaking for me seeing other women pregnant and reading about children being abandoned or abused because they were not wanted. I sat there wondering why these people were given children they didn't want when I wanted a child so badly it hurt.

I had to have surgery 18 years ago, and while the doctor was doing the procedure, he found out why I could not get pregnant and fixed the problem. Two months later, I figured I was coming down with the flu because I was sick to my stomach. I went to the doctor, and since it had been over a year since my last visit, he did a pregnancy test before prescribing my medicine. One nurse had just finished taking a vial of blood when another nurse came in and told me the pregnancy test had come back positive. I stared at her as if she had grown another head and asked her if she were sure it was positive. When she said, "Yes," I started crying. She misunderstood and thought I was upset until I told her we had been trying for 18 years to have a baby and that those tears were of happiness and joy. My happiness and joy is now a 17-year-old, 6-foot-tall young man getting ready to go out into the world. I can guarantee I will cry when he leaves the nest.

Mrs. Jennifer Bellanger

SOMETIMES WE PRAY

Sometimes we pray

And don't really believe

The Lord our God

Is able to see

Our hurts and pains

And all we're going through

Our Father in heaven

Has already devised a plan

Just adhere to His Word

And follow His commands

We will began to see

Everything in His hands

So whenever you pray

Don't ever doubt

That the Lord our God

Will not fail to carry you out.

§

What has made me weep was my mother's inability to accept me. For a long time, I felt as if I were a failure. All of my brothers and sisters went to college and obtained degrees. I was not college material, so I entered the military and made it a career. My mother looked down on me because I did not have a degree, and it came to a point where I stopped attending family functions. My brothers and sisters missed me, so I started having family functions at my house. I invited my mother, but I instructed her that we would not discuss my lack of a college education. I had endured my mother's abuse for years, and I told her I was not going to stand for it anymore. She finally accepted me for who I am.

Anonymous

ALWAYS

BE

YOURSELF

WHEN YOU BECOME SOMEONE ELSE

THERE WILL BE A PROBLEM.

§

Like most girls, I had a plan for my life. I was going to go to college, get married, and have two children. This was my dream and I was going to live it. As the years began to slip by, I realized that I was not interested in college, and I had not met the man of my dreams who was going to be the father of my children. The only time I really thought about these things was around my birthday. I would become a little depressed, but then after a while, I would shake it off and move on.

On my 28th birthday, I finally understood that this dream of mine was not going to happen. I was depressed for a while, but this time, I could not shake it off. I cried daily. After feeling sorry for myself and talking to my best friend daily about this, I realized that I was angry at God for not making my dreams come true. I learned that the dreams that the Lord had for me were so much higher than the ones I had for myself. I didn't give up my dreams, but I began to understand that I needed to be open to the fact that what I had been planning may not be what God was planning for me. The next year on my birthday I was not depressed. I was very content with the knowledge that God had a perfect plan and purpose for my life. Today, I am 41-years-old; I am unmarried; and I have not finished college. I absolutely do not want children. I am a partner with my best friends, running a business that I love, and I am considering going to culinary school. I remain content where God has placed me.

Carla Brown

§

This is the story of RH. She had a close friend who I will call Nikki. Her friend had two teenage children and was going through financial difficulties and asked for a loan. Nikki promised to pay the loan back in two months, but RH gave her three months to pay it back. After six months and many unsuccessful attempts to call Nikki at home, RH came to the conclusion that she had been played. Nikki's phone was no longer receiving calls. RH was hurt because she tried to help a friend who was in need, but when it was time for her friend to live up to her word, she failed to do so. RH now says that it is painful when you can't even trust friends. Her heart bleeds and she cries.

A TRUE FRIEND

A true friend is hard to find

You have my back all the time

Even when I cannot find my way

You always know the right words to say

Sometimes you say words

I don't want to hear

But you tell the truth

Because you really care

Thank you for being a true friend

Weeping endures for a night: but joy comes in the morning!

Psalm 30:5

§

In 1996, my mother was diagnosed with breast cancer. While she was going through her treatment, my husband decided that he wanted to leave me. I had just had our second daughter about five months before, and his decision was a huge blow to me. During our separation, my mother died. In August 1997, my divorce was final. A few months later, I found out I was adopted after 35 years. In October, my house went into foreclosure. I was blessed to sell it in one hour, but I had to file bankruptcy and lost my car. I moved in with a friend, but she later put me and my children out on the street, so we were homeless for about two weeks.

After all I went through; you would have thought these things would have made me cry. One day, shortly after I moved into my own place, I was working out and talking to God. The conversation went something like this: "God, all I want is someone that I can depend on, someone that I know is going to be there for me. I just want to go to sleep at night and not worry about anything. God that is all I want." God spoke to me and said, "I have been here all the time." I broke out crying because for the first time in my life I finally realized that all I ever needed was God, and He had been there all the time. That was the day my life changed, and I have never been the same.

From that point on, when I cry, I cry out to God because I know that He is the only one who can change things in my life. He is always there and I can sleep at night and not have to worry about anything. I know I can depend on Him. Like the Scripture says, "My help comes from the Lord."

Gleneice Hopson

I SURVIVED

I survived

Through thick and thin

And all the chaos

In between

It was by His grace

The idea

I could see His face

In the special place

You know

On the throne

In His heavenly home

In that place called Heaven

Streets filled with gold

Angels walking tall

Talking to God

I survived

The unexplained

All the crazy games

I survived.

§

First Comes Weeping, Then Comes Joy

My husband and I lived in separate states because of a failed real estate deal, and his job required him to travel a lot. It was one month shy of our 17th anniversary. He e-mailed and said, "Tonya, I want a divorce. And I don't want to argue about something that I already made my mind up about." I knew something was wrong and had known for some time. He did not call me. He did not even call his children. No anniversary card and no Valentine's goodies were sent. I did not have proof of infidelity, but I knew that something was missing. Was it the tragic, life-shattering events that we had just experienced in our lives? Was it the argument that we had a month ago? Was it another female? Was it me?

So many unanswered questions. How could this happen? We were both ministers of the Gospel. We vowed to death do us part. We had written one-, three-, and five-year plans. We had prayed and counseled other couples. We had witnessed God working miracles in other marriages. We planned to retire in a few years, so we could travel. We had plans for our ministry. We had created businesses. Were we ever really one? How long had my husband lived a lie? Was he still saved or had he backslidden? Here is a fact: There are numerous Christians who walk around in denial because they are spiritually sick and weak in God and hide it. Here is a truth: Jesus is a healer.

At first, that e-mail knocked the life out of me. I am a strong woman of God, but for a few days, I lost my mind. For three days, I did not eat or sleep. Day and night, all I did was cry. I prayed and asked God for a word, a vision, anything. Normally, I do not allow my children to sleep at other people's houses, but that weekend I let them go. I could not bear to let them see me in that weakened state of body, soul, and spirit. I really lived that Scripture in Job that says, "I have treasured the words of His mouth more than my necessary food" (Job 23:12b). Finally, God said, "Weeping may endure for a night, but joy comes in the morning" (Ps 30:5b). Also, God said, "No divorce; I got my son."

24

It has only been a couple of months since that e-mail, but I am stronger and wiser. I have made up in my mind that the enemy will not have my joy, my godly marriage, my three godly children, my ministry, and my businesses. For 40 days, I fasted and prayed. At the end of the fast, God assured me that I would have the petitions of my heart. I am praising God for permanent, complete deliverance and healing for me and my family. I am thanking God for teaching me about unconditional love, forgiveness, peace, and joy. Also, He is teaching me about me and changing me. I am thanking God for empowering me and showing me that He is my source, not my husband. Many times in the past, God has given me a word. He always made it happen. So it is with my marriage, my future, and my family. God has my husband's heart and mind in His hands. No worries, just faith and belief in God. I can hear Anita Baker singing, "There will be no more tears . . ." I have my joy back now.

Tonya

LIFE IS A TRIP

Life is a trip

At some stops

You will glide smoothly and easily

At other stops

It will be bumpy and hard.

Whatever the situation

Keep moving until you reach your destination

Look forward

Don't look back.

§

I have cried many times. And in those times of pain, I often lamented and felt sorry for myself, whether a situation was caused by my own doing or by the hand of another. "Why do I have to experience this pain?" I would ask. "What is it that God is trying to get me to learn?" I would say to myself. This is not fair I would conclude.

Thinking back, I know I have had many teachable moments that I possibly would have missed if it were not for the pain I experienced. For instance, I would have missed THE important lesson about the precious gift of life. I would have taken for granted the fact that giving life to another is actually a gift that is not guaranteed to all. You see, like most young women, I had my life plan mapped out. I knew that I was going to go to school, get married, and have a family of my own one day. And for the most part, things progressed according to *my* plan. I entered and graduated from a prestigious university, had a supportive family, had a wonderful group of friends, and met a wonderful man and married him.

As a married couple, we lived a wonderful life full of experiences that one could only dream of and we seemed to have it all. He was a professional athlete, and I was a young nurse caring for sick children. We were on top of the world. Anything that we wanted was ours. We traveled from coast to coast, city to city, restaurant to restaurant. Whatever we wanted, it was there for us until the moment came when that all changed. Like many other couples, we decided after a couple of years of marriage that it was time to begin a family. So naturally, we tried and tried and tried and tried . . . with no success. I could not get pregnant, although everyone around me could get pregnant. Everywhere I looked, I saw pregnant females. The teenager down the street was pregnant. My friend with no husband was pregnant. My friend with a husband was pregnant. The lady at the grocery store was pregnant. I even think the dog across the street was pregnant, but I was not pregnant!

Everyone was pregnant but me! How could this be happening to me? I thought. I have never wanted for anything and not gotten it, I told myself. This is not right, I concluded. After a year of trying, we decided that we needed to accept the fact that something may be wrong, so we went to get checked out. Actually, there is a funny story about how our checking out began. My husband played professional sports, so naturally he went to the trainer for advice on where to get help for our problem. The trainer pointed him in a direction, and off we went to the doctor's office as a couple to get checked. However, no questions were being asked of me, but only of my husband. I thought that was odd, although we soon learned that we were at a urology appointment and not a fertility specialist when the doctor asked my husband to drop his pants to be examined. It was really funny to see a grown man's face turn gray at the thought of what was going to happen to him. Thankfully, my husband "took one for the team." He got through his rectal exam as well as a series of other tests with no problems. Eventually, we found out that he was fine, which meant that I was the problem. Guess what? I cried!

After all the time we tried to have a child to no avail, we finally found out that I was the one with the problem. Why me? Why me? Why me? My mantra was "I JUST WANT TO BE NORMAL!!!!" However, normal I was not. Upon discovering that my ovulation capability was out of whack, I was placed on fertility medicine that made me crazy! It made my husband crazy too. I was premenopausal 24 hours a day, 7 days a week. I felt as if I were a young woman in an older woman's body. I had night sweats and hot flashes, and the mood swings were awful. It was so bad that it was difficult to be around me. After six months of fertility treatments with no pregnancy in sight, we had to explore more interventions to help me become pregnant.

Eventually, we were offered the opportunity to have artificial insemination using my husband's sperm. Although this was not ideal for me, my husband thought it was pretty cool. So, off to the little tiny room in the fertility specialist's office we went to provide our specimens for the procedure. I am happy to admit that this procedure was a success, and we found out I was pregnant one month later. I cried when the pregnancy test stick turned blue because I almost didn't believe my eyes because so many before had not changed color. We cried at the thought that our dream would become a reality. We were finally going to have our own baby!

The pregnancy was wonderful. I was never sick. I gained the perfect amount of weight, and the baby progressed wonderfully. I had the most beautiful baby shower ever! And after nine months, I was ready to have our baby. The day I went into labor was fun. After my water broke, I went to a baseball game to watch my husband play, not realizing that I would leak throughout the game. Actually at the game, I had to borrow another friend's shirt to cover my bottom and prevent showing that I was soon going to deliver a baby based on the wet spot on my shorts.

After I went into labor, my baby did not want to come out! After 19 hours of labor, it was decided that I would need to have a c-section to expedite the process. We wanted to see our baby boy, so my husband and I agreed. What we found out when our son was born was something we were not prepared for at all.

When my son was born, we immediately knew something was wrong. When he looked at us, we saw opaque blue eyes when his eyes should have been clear brown. He could not see us. His eyes were cloudy due to a condition known as congenital glaucoma. I am a nurse, and I had never heard of a child having glaucoma. Here we were with a baby who could not look back at us because his eye pressure was so high that his corneas were clouded over. Looking at his eyes, you would have thought you were looking at a 100-year-old's eyes. My heart was broken! I cried for the uncertainty that we faced. I cried for the pain that my son faced. I cried, "This is not fair! Why my baby? Why us? We tried so hard to have this baby, and now he will be faced with this pain." This was so unfair I thought.

I cried for my poor baby son and the pain he was experiencing. I cried for the double eye surgery he had at three days old. I cried for the five more he had that never seemed to keep the pressure down. I cried when the doctors told us that there was nothing they could do. I cried when they told me that the best we could hope for was for him to see large letters. I cried at the possibility of him being rendered legally blind. As I looked up at the clear, crisp blue sky, I felt the pain of knowing that he may never see this wondrous sight. Why him? Why our little bundle of joy? He did not deserve this. This was so unfair . . . I just wanted to take this from him. "God, please let it be me instead," I cried. We continually prayed for a miracle, asking God to please help us through this troubling time. We were faithful and uncertain at the same time.

However, once we thought there was nothing else we could do, we received a suggestion from one of the doctors to visit a doctor in Boston who specialized in congenital glaucoma. We contacted him right away, and we cried at the possibility of hope. He told us he would see us right away, and we told him we would be there the next day. We made the five-hour trip to find a way to give our precious baby the gift of sight. The doctor knew exactly what our son needed and started a new course of treatment right away. After about a month or two of being on a new medicine to keep the eye pressure down, our son went into surgery again to have permanent tubes placed in his eyes so the pressure could be relieved mechanically. The procedure worked, but we had to monitor him very closely to make sure his eye pressure remained under control. We had to travel back and forth from our home five hours away every week and often had to stay in Boston for weeks at a time to make sure his eye pressure would remain stable. It was not an easy road, and he required several surgeries and lots of follow up. Over the course of the first two years of his life, he had a total of 12 eye surgeries. However, he was a trooper.

I am happy to report that our baby is now 8-years-old, and he is outstanding! I cry at the thought of how wonderful he is doing. He wears glasses and he can see with them! He is a normal little boy. He plays baseball and he is good at it too! He is very kindhearted. He has such a gentle nature, and he is a true blessing from God. When I look at my son, I see the gift of life that I longed so much for, for so long. I appreciate the pain that I experienced in trying to bring him into this world, and I thank my son for the important lesson he taught me about the precious gift of life. I thank him for helping me to appreciate life's special gifts. I pray that I will always remember the lessons of his life every time I look at him. I am happy it was me who was blessed to travel along this journey with him. I thank God for this tremendous lesson of life and love.

Melissa Gomes, PhD, RN

THE UNKNOWN

Sometimes the serenity

Quiets me

And I think

About the unknown

That is forever present

And close by

Reminding me

That something is about to happen.

§

We weep because of various reasons:

We cry because we love someone who passed away

We cry because we love someone who does not love us back the way we want them to

We cry because we are happy and joyful about a blessed event in our lives . . . i.e., birth of a newborn baby

We cry at weddings

We cry at movies, sad stories, or happy endings in a love story

We cry because we reflect on how good God has been to us with His mercy and favor

We cry because we have been beaten

Patricia Alston

§

Just an ordinary day I thought while I was busy cleaning and humming the tune to a very familiar worship song. My peaceful tranquility was then disrupted by a single phone call. A stranger on the opposite line asked, "Ms. Holly?" "Yes," I replied trying to connect the voice to a face. The stranger said, "The policeman arrested Jay and brought him to jail, and the bond is 10,000.00 . . ."

Living a good life and teaching morals and godliness to my son were not enough to steer him from trouble. One lesson I learned, first and foremost, was he himself needed a personal relationship with the Creator. He needed to be fully aware that he was loved regardless of the circumstance(s). Letters sent to him with expressions of love were encouraging; words of self-worthiness were empowering; and Scriptures accompanied with interpretations were enlightening to an imprisoned soul. An awesome God taught me more than a few lessons during this trying time.

Grievously and with overwhelming despondency, I thrust my fatigued body to the floor and cried out to the Lord. After having travailed for a lengthy time, a soft tapping on my shoulder caused me to pause and then a soft, peaceful, and assuring voice whispered, "If you do not believe, stop praying. God has not lost control, and He wants you to walk before Him in faith. You need to have radical faith that breaks the barrel of all odds."

An artist once sang that God specializes in things that seem impossible; but, I am a witness to a greater truth: God specializes in things that *are* impossible. Meanwhile, the God of mercy and comfort was visiting my son who was feeling very suicidal for having been falsely arrested and cast into lockdown for losing his temper. My son wrote these words, "Mother, Jesus visited me today. I was indescribably angry, crying out of control,

and fearful. I wanted to end my life. And I could feel a presence—a sweet peace and calmest, that words cannot describe, came over me. I wasn't alone; for, I know Jesus was with me. Again I started to sob out of control;

but, this time the tears released all the anguish and fear. And knowing I was innocent the thought came to mind that perhaps God allowed me to go through this to get my attention." Praise the mighty name of the Lord!

Holly A. Winston

TRUST HIM

It is at these times
When we are at the lowest we can go
The valley is dark and deep
And there is no light to behold

I have to trust in God
And believe in His unconditional love
He will surely pull me through
And show me what I need to do

Doing what is right in His sight
Doing whatever is His will
Is the only way I can live
But I have to be willing to give
One hundred percent and truly believe

That is I put my trust in Him
He will prove to me again and again
That He is the King of Kings
And my everything
Put your trust in Him!

§

Weeping for me is a rarity. I save it for special occasions. But, when it comes it's like Niagra Falls—noise and all.

As a single mother raising a young daughter, there were many times I squelched my tears. I didn't want my daughter to see how dire I thought our circumstances were because the world is tough enough, and kids shouldn't have to worry about their basic needs being met. I can remember holding it in until she wasn't in the house or silently crying into my pillow at night. I cried because I worried—worried about not having enough to pay the mortgage or the monthly utility bills. I cried because I was dealing with problems on the job, issues at the school, car repairs, home repairs, and on, and on, and on.

I had just enough money to make ends meet, nothing extra for a busted water pipe or car transmission repair. I couldn't afford to get sick because I couldn't afford the deductible. And later—much later—I found out that a cash-till-payday loan is nothing more than legal loan-sharking. I ended up in an endless, nightmarish cycle with another bill to pay. The stretching of my paycheck continued from one week to the next with the weeks and months stretching into two years. But, nevertheless, I pressed forward. I held on and prayed and told myself, "It's going to get better; it's going to *be* better—next year!"

I can remember as a teenager how I dreamed of marrying in my mid-20s, having two or three children, and having them all in college by my mid-40s; however, by the age of 41 I was still a single mother with a 13-year-old and married to my job. My daughter had a better social life than I had. My Friday night consisted of dropping my daughter off at one of her friend's homes and coming back to watch a movie with my dog. It was definitely not the life I envisioned . . . or wanted. I cried from loneliness, frustration, and financial instability. I wanted someone to share my life with—I wanted my childhood dream or at least a part of it.

Two years ago, at the age of 42, my dream came true. I married a wonderful man from my church who had a 13-year-old son and 9-year-old daughter. The odd part was I didn't meet him at church. I met him through a dating service! Our congregation was so large that there was a Saturday evening service and three Sunday services. He attended the Saturday service, and I attended the second Sunday service. As it turned out, I needed to take a good look at how I lived my life. Along the way, I realized I needed to have more faith in my prayers. Psalm 37:4 reads, "Delight yourself in the Lord and he will give you the desires of your heart." It is a Scripture that I continue to trust and believe.

Angela Seward

PEACE, JOY, AND LOVE

Peace

All around me

In me

Saturating my soul

Joy

A gift from God

Exhilarating

Stimulating

Love

Caressing me

Completing me

Filling me up

The greatest gift of all.

§

There is no incident in particular that comes to mind that would make me weep in regard to despair, lost love, etc. I do know the pain of losing a loved one and the feeling of the pain being so strong and overwhelming that you feel as though you can't make it. Breathing, let alone weeping, is impossible. But when the weeping comes, it's like a flood wall of tears, and you cry so long and so hard it actually hurts your heart. This type of weeping is so intense that when you are finished, your head hurts and your eyes are swollen; hopefully, no one sees you in that condition. The only one you have to lean on during an episode of this magnitude is God. He is the only one who understands that kind of loss, the only one who can heal that kind of hurt, the only one who can alleviate that kind of pain. So when the crying jag is over, you fall to your knees, and you call upon the only one who will hear and answer your call . . . God.

CW

§

Throughout my daughter's formative years, I regularly taught her about the dangers and consequences of drug use. Unfortunately, I did not tell her that I used drugs as a senior in high school. One day after school when my daughter was in the eighth grade, she and a friend stopped in a neighborhood coffee shop and met a guy I knew in high school. During a casual conversation, he overheard her mention my alma mater. He asked her my name, and he told her, "Oh, I know Karen. We used to smoke weed together." My daughter was crushed. After she told me about the incident later that evening, I was devastated. She asked me outright if what he said was true, and, of course, I acknowledged that it was the truth. She broke out in tears, and so did I. I apologized to her for not telling her earlier.

I now tell my daughter any and everything I can think of about my past—no matter how ugly it is to me. I was disgusted that she would learn something like this from such an insensitive person. This incident reminded me that trust and honesty are important when developing parent-child relationships.

TRUTH

The truth is

Pure

Powerful

Honest

Desired

Wanted

Needed

Truth should be

Woven into your soul

Instilled in your heart

Meditated on

Told often

Pondered upon

And a constant in your life

And relationships.

§

Two thousand and five was a very rough year for me, starting in August 2005 when Hurricane Katrina came through and hit my beloved city of New Orleans. I cried for about a week, especially after I saw a man on CNN who told the reporter that he had just lost his wife. I will never forget how helpless I felt being in Virginia and not being able to help my people, and the people of New Orleans are truly my people. Of course, I didn't know all of them personally, but I knew their areas and that could have been me, helpless and in need of a way to safety. My aunt lived near the St. Bernard projects in New Orleans, and thank God, she left one day before the hurricane hit. It took my aunt, her husband, and her dog 12 hours to go 50 miles west of New Orleans to Paulina, Louisiana. She was safe but her house was destroyed, and everything she worked so hard for all of her life was gone. My aunt and uncle were able to live in my mother's house in Paulina, Louisiana. The house was vacant because my mother was living in a nursing home in Houston, Texas, because she was recovering from a stroke she suffered in 2001.

On Thanksgiving Day in 2005, right before I was about to put my turkey in the oven, I got a call from my sister saying that my father had died from cancer. I cried that day, not for him, but for the relationship we never had and will never have. I cried for a man I didn't know; I cried for a man who I was not sure if I loved; and I cried for a man who I will never be sure loved me. I cried and cried and cried because a piece of my family history was gone, and my son will never get to know his grandfather. I always hoped that he would be a grandfather to my child, even though he was never a father to me. Well, that day I never finished my Thanksgiving dinner, and my family and I went to have dinner with my neighbors and very special friends.

I went back to Lutcher, Louisiana, for my father's funeral to pay my last respects and to get closure on a relationship that was never formed and that will never happen. I went to show forgiveness; I went to show respect; and I went to show love for a man I didn't even know or for most of my younger years didn't even like. Forgiveness is a powerful action and word.

While attending my father's funeral, I also had to worry about my mother, who was in the hospital in Houston, Texas. My older sister and I drove from Houston, Texas, to Lutcher, Louisiana, to attend my father's funeral. The entire time we were at the funeral we worried about our mother. Thirteen days after my father died, my mother passed away. I have never cried so much in my life. It was December 8, 2008, and it was a day I couldn't stop crying. I was on I-95 heading to work in Washington, DC, when I got the phone call from my sister saying that my mother didn't make it. The first thing I did was pull on the side of the road. I called my friend Janice and asked her what day it was and she told me December 8, 2005. I told her that my mother had just died. I then talked to my husband and my brother-in-law to confirm that I was not having a nightmare, and they confirmed that my mother and friend was gone forever.

I'm crying right now as I write this because my mother was everything to me and my sisters: she was our friend, father, provider, mentor, and sometimes our enemy. She and I had a great daughter-mother relationship, and she was very supportive of me joining the Navy. I loved her so much, and I know she loved me. The day she died forever changed my life, but her death never changed the wonderful memories I have of her gumbo, mustard greens, and cabbage. Her death also never changed the fact that she was forever a size 6 and loved to wear high heels and makeup.

My mother leaving me that day is still unbelievable, and when I think about her and how much I miss her, I still cry. I'm getting ready to retire from the Navy, and I know she would be very proud of me. She and I had plans to go on a cruise together to celebrate my retirement. I am going to cry when I retire, not for me, but for her because she will not be there to share this special moment. I guess the last time I cried was today, February 13, 2009, for Mrs. Dorothy Mae Joseph of Paulina, Louisiana.

Cassandra Brown-Coney

A MOTHER'S LOVE

A mother's love is irreplaceable

Can never be erased

Will never fade

Always remains true

No matter what you do

Her love for you can never be broken

Cannot be stolen

Never gets old

Pure like 24-karat gold

A mother's love is

Always and forever.

§

Life itself offers many reasons to weep. It is not always under our control, but rather life dictates many things to us that we truly do not ask to come our way. I would like to share the happy things that have made me weep.

I gave birth to a son and a daughter, in just that order, which God blessed me to walk with Him during a very formative part of their lives. When they arrived, I was so happy—"I wept."

My granddaughter was born with a cleft lip and palate, and three surgeries later, she called me "Grandma." Now she is 14-years-old. When I hear her voice, the sound of her voice brings happiness into my heart. When I watch my granddaughter and my husband play checkers and accuse each other of cheating, it is a funny sight to see, so I begin to thank God for the sight of it all—"I weep."

When I go to church on Sundays after having one hell of a week and hear Pastor Riddick preach words from God Himself to me, I feel my soul respond with joy—"I weep." When I hang out with my friends and family and we are all laughing, playing games, and acting silly, I go home and thank God for the time I shared with them—"I weep."

When my mind tries to remind me of all the things I do not have, my spirit speaks to me to remind me of all I do have, such as the ability to walk, to see, to talk, to hear, and to dance. I have the ability to get wealth and bless others along the way. I have a sound mind and the gift of expressing my feelings through the written word. I have the freedom of self-expression in a world where many do not have that privilege, and many who do have it, never use it. I think of the life God has given me, so many more happy times than unhappy times. Some women weep from the happiness of just thinking about the joy God has given them. I can only speak for myself, but I would not trade my joy for all the tea in China or anywhere else for that matter. I weep with joy, I weep.

Phyllis L. Jones (A happy weeper)

THANKSGIVING PRAYER

There is so much for me to be thankful for

My family, my friends, my Lord who loves me

The blood that was shed on Calvary

The angels that are constantly protecting me

His grace and mercy that guides forever

No weapons bought against me shall prevail

Even though they slay me-my spirit will not fail

The prayer partners who continue to lift me up

The preachers and Saints who bring the word

I am grateful and humbly thankful

§

As a little girl, my little sister, cousins, and I always went to Grandma's (my maternal grandmother) house for the summer. She lives in a rural part of South Carolina, so there was plenty of space for the grandchildren to play and run around. While the other kids were playing and causing trouble, I was always with Grandma in the house, cooking, watching television, or going to the town to shop. I loved hanging out with "Mrs. Thelma." She would teach me all the little secrets there are to know about being a woman. She was even teaching me when I thought we were just playing. Two years ago, my grandmother was diagnosed with Alzheimer's disease, and this was devastating to our family. The diagnosis affected me to the point where I had to drop out of nursing school for a semester. Not only did I cry, but I fell into a state of depression. Watching the health of the backbone of our family deteriorate mentally and physically causes excruciating pain.

After missing a semester of school, I decided that leaving school wasn't the best option. My grandmother in her right mind would not have approved of me being a college dropout, so I moved from the University of South Carolina and started over in Hampton, Virginia. My grandmother is my driving force for becoming a nurse. I will graduate on December 19, 2008, and on that day I will feel proud and accomplished for more than one reason.

Hermanda Prioleau

Sometimes hope

is all we have . . . .

It's all we need . . .

Live life to the fullest

And then

Live some more.

§

My name is Shyla Miles, and I am in the process of writing my testimony. At such a young age, I have experienced things that a lot of people would have a hard time understanding. Of course everyone has a story to tell, but honestly speaking, the only story that truly matters is the one told that has a purpose. No one wants to hear of your hard times if you haven't overcome them, and no one wants to hear of your successes if you've never had hard times. So throughout this story, you will hear about my hard times and successes.

I experienced my lowest points as an adopted child, always feeling insecure and out of place. Even with my childhood insecurities, I still managed to grow, accomplish goals, and become a mature, confident, yet, humble young woman. The truth is I haven't been the first to witness hardships in life, and I won't be the last. My purpose isn't to try to convince you that my journey is better or worse than anyone else's; this is written simply to let others know they're not alone. You cannot run from life's struggles, but with a little help, you can walk through them with ease. Unfortunately, the world believes that wisdom only comes with age. Well, I am here to tell you that wisdom comes with experience, and I am living proof that experience has no age limit! Life is about choice, not chance, and the longer it takes for you to accept this, the longer it will take for you to reach your destiny.

Weeping, weeping, weeping . . . .

§

Did you ever think your parents would live forever? One of the worst heartaches in life is when they die. You feel as though you're in limbo. The two people who were constants in your life are no longer there for you to turn to when you're troubled by some situation or when trouble comes into your life. When they were here, you had someone to comfort you and pray for you.

In August 2007, my 91-year-old mother told me how much she loved me and tried to give me all of her jewelry and some of her clothing. She also told me that her Captain (Jesus) had come, and He was taking her with Him and she was ready to go. Three weeks later, she was gone. She died a beautiful death—very peaceful.

In July 2008, my older brother Calvin, a double amputee, was very tired of the pacemaker and defibrillator that kept him here and he also went on to glory. On August 20, 2008, at 4:30 am, I received a phone call from the Lafourche Parish Sheriff's Office telling me that my youngest sister was dead. She was killed in the line of duty. It felt as though someone had pierced my heart with an arrow. All I could do was fall to my knees and scream, "No! No! No!" I was thinking that with Mom and Dad gone I was supposed to help take care of my younger siblings.

I know in my heart that I will see my sister again, but right now, I'm still waiting for her to call. As I sit by the phone, the tears fall from my eyes at will and without warning. I know God is with me because without Him to comfort me I would be in a deep depression. To add to all who died in my family, my husband's nephew, his niece, and his younger brother also died within a span of three months of one another. I will press on until the day I am reunited with my family.

Mrs. Edith Scoby

WAITING

Waiting

Patiently

Quietly

For the answers

To the questions

I have asked

Expecting

Anticipating

Hoping that your answers

Will be favorable

And true

Listening

Comprehending

Understanding

Knowing that

Whatever the outcome may be

I will accept it and go on

§

Women weep for many reasons. Sometimes women weep out of sadness, other times tears are shed out of joy. It is also not uncommon for women to cry in frustration and anger. Every now and then, women have been known to cry for no particular reason; for example, observe the tears that can be produced in response to a "Hallmark" commercial.

The tears of a mother are often generated in response to situations involving her children. As a mother myself, I hold most dear my relationship with my children. Anything that hurts them hurts me. Anything that keeps them from me hurts me. On the positive side, things that bring them joy and happiness tend to bring out the same in me. All of these things, whether good or bad, can bring me to tears. These are a few of the reasons women weep.

We cry when we lose the people who we love-but in our hearts we know God has them in the palm of His hands.

§

Crying is a form of release. A girl always feels better after a good cry. Lots of things have made me weep over the years—the births of my sons, the passing of loved ones, and the love of my God. During my quiet times with the Lord, I have often been lead to tears. The tears come from the unconditional love that He has for me. God doesn't pass judgment on us, and He gives us what He promises. He doesn't let us down in our time of need and comfort.

Recently, I was at an amazing funeral. Tons of family, friends, and loved ones came out to pay their respects to an incredible lady. I wept a little during the service, but it was at the gravesite that I cried. Now, I am sure you are thinking I cried at her gravesite. But no, I didn't cry there. As the funeral goers gathered to say their last good-byes, I stayed in the distance—I don't do the whole walking on the dead thing.

Nearby, I noticed a young man. He was walking across the rows of the resting, clearly in search of something. This young man came to his final stop. He cleared the debris off a marker and stood alone in silence on this chilly day. I knew this young man. He is the same age as my son, and they grew up playing sports together. His father was an amazing man and a wonderful coach to so many young men. As I watched him, tears began to come down my face uncontrollably. I thought what a fine young man he was and how difficult it must be to continue to play sports, graduate from high school, and now go off to college without his father. At that moment, my heart broke. As he walked back across the maze of markers, he found me. I don't know how our eyes met, but they did. This young man, without saying one single word to me, taught me a little about love and a lot about thankfulness that day. I wept with him in my arms.

Shari Wilson

If Jesus wept–so will we . . . .

§

What makes me weep is when a woman with no self-esteem lets a man tell her for eight years that he is going to leave his wife for her. Over a period of eight years, the woman falls in love with the man and puts her life on hold. When she hears a song on the radio, she calls the wife and tells her that she is in love with her husband. She demands that the wife get out of bed and meet her somewhere. "And what will we discuss?" the wife asks. The woman tells the wife that she knows many things about her and she does. The husband has betrayed the wife and told the woman personal things about his wife that only a person who lives in the husband and wife's house could have known. The woman is hurt, and she wants the wife to hurt and feel sympathy for her. She proceeds to tell the wife that she will send her things in the mail that the husband has given her over the years. And, yes, she sends those things to the wife.

What makes the wife weep is the husband has an affair with is a brainless twit. The woman has three children by three different men. Obviously, the woman has low self-esteem, doesn't value herself, and does not fear God. What makes the wife weep is that she has to tell the woman she should be setting a good example for her daughters. What does the woman tell her daughters when they ask, "Why does Mr. _____ have to go home to his wife every night?" What does the woman tell her children when she must spend every holiday alone? What makes the wife weep is that the woman tells her, "I need to pray, but I don't." What makes the wife weep is that in 2010 women still believe a man when he says that he is not happy at home and he will leave his wife. But come on people, eight years? I am crying and laughing at the stupidity of this woman—WOW!

YOU HAVE SOWN BAD SEEDS

You have sown bad seeds

Lies

Deception

Betrayal

Dishonesty

You will reap what you have sown

Deceit

Corruption

Bitterness

Death

§§

I have wept many times. I cry when I'm happy or sad. I cry when I'm upset and when I am disappointed. I cry in church in adoration of God. I have cried out of joy as I celebrated my 20th wedding anniversary and the births of my children. The most noteworthy tears have come as a result of pain, not just typical pain like the kind you feel from shutting your finger in the door, but the kind of pain that causes feelings of desperation. It's the kind of pain that makes you feel hopeless and gives you no alternative but to face the inevitable. Both of my parents have passed away. Although the loss of my mother was the most dreadful thing that I ever experienced, it wasn't until my father passed away five years later that I realized I had learned something in the process.

I remember visiting my father the day before he passed away. He had just had surgery, and things did not look good. As I rode to the hospital, I remember tears rolling down my face. I knew in my heart that he was not going to make it. As I turned on the radio, I heard a song that I knew God sent me from heaven: "I Need You Now" by Smokie Norful. I heard the Holy Spirit say, "Let him go" and that is when my heart broke into pieces. I asked, "Let him go? How can I just let my father go?" I finished letting the song minister to me. I did not know what I was to say when I went into the hospital, so I asked the Lord to put words in my mouth and to encourage my heart.

As I entered my father's hospital room, I felt a sense of peace—the kind that surpasses all understanding. I knew where it came from, and I went over to his bed and he turned and looked at me. I opened my mouth and God did the rest. My heart was heavy as I told my father more than just the usual "I love you." I shared with him what a wonderful man he was to me. I also expressed to him that I knew he was tired, and we (my siblings and I) would be okay. He could rest now. The next day my father left this world for a better place. I knew that although what I did was difficult, I had done the will of the Lord. Weeping is a healthy release and to everything there is a season. Since that day, two of my siblings have passed away, and now I can say death does not have to leave you hopeless. We should all live this life in such a way that we will one day rise and live again.

Anita Bonner

We know God will wipe all of our tears away.

§

I have had some very trying and hard times in my life that have made me cry. The one that sticks out the most is the day that my brother Gerald Murphy Bush was killed in an 18 wheeler accident in Atlanta, GA. He was the youngest of five children born to Mr. and Mrs. Murphy Bush Sr. Even though it has almost been 10 years since the accident, it seems as though it was just yesterday. It was May 21, 1999, and I was working at the Department of Public Works. My mother called the office at approximately 9:00 am, and she told my coworkers not to tell me. They told me there was an emergency, and I needed to get home.

I didn't know what to think. I was driving home thinking all sorts of things. When I reached home, my mother and our next-door neighbor were outside talking. When I got out of the car, she called me inside. She asked me if I loved her, and I told her, "Yes." I said, "Mom what is the matter?" She then told me that my baby brother was killed early that morning in a car accident. I did not cry at that moment because it did not hit me then, so I went to my room. I began to think about all the times me and my brother spent together growing up. He was three years younger than me, and we shared everything. We were very close. I did not believe he was dead because we talked every day, and I just thought that he would call me later. I began to ponder our conversation the day before when he told me he was coming down for the summer.

As the day of the funeral approached, I was still in denial that he was dead. I had to see for myself that my baby brother was gone. When I walked in the church and saw him lying in that coffin, I just broke down and cried. That was the worst day of my life. I still think of that day, and I cry because I cannot talk to him anymore. He was my ace. He left behind three children, two boys and one girl. His daughter was only five-years-old, but she remembers everything about her dad. All of his children have very vivid memories of their father, and this makes me happy because they are all good memories. I often cry on his birthday and at Christmas because he came home.

Juanesta Bush

§

Sometimes I weep because I am so blessed it is unreal. The little things I endure are nothing compared to the things that are endured by people who are hungry, homeless, penniless, and do not know God. I have never been hungry. I have more than enough food in my refrigerator. You can look at my size and see I have never missed a meal, a snack, or an aroma. I have been blessed to buy lunch for my friends when their money is short. My house is safe and warm, and when it is 20 degrees outside, I do not have to live in a cardboard box. I have clean, warm clothes, and I sleep on a great mattress. I am not standing outside of Wal-Mart with a sign that reads, "Will work for food or money." I have a job, and I go to that job every day the Lord sees fit to open my eyes, give me strength, and provide me with a sound mind. I have the opportunity to live in a country where you can praise God any way you see fit. I can praise God any time I want, wherever I want, and in any manner I want. My church does not dictate that you wear certain clothes—the pastor just wants you to show up and be blessed. And you know what? I am blessed. And that, my friends, is enough to make anyone weep tears of joy.

Alfreada Brown-Kelly

One thing that makes me weep is the way God continuously
bless me even when I fall short.

§

Working with abused children can wreak havoc on your soul. One child was 10-years-old and had been forced to leave school. She was taking care of the household, and her father was molesting her every chance he could get. This made me weep uncontrollably, because for the most part, women do not engage in sexual intercourse until they are mature enough to handle the situation. So when I think about this innocent child, who was forced into the lifestyle of a woman, I cringe. A 10-year-old cannot grasp the concept of making love, and I wanted to do things to that man that were unspeakable. Working with abused and neglected kids will tear your soul apart. When you think you have seen it all, something else happens that is worse than the last thing. We must protect the children. Adults who hurt children—physically, mentally, and verbally—should be punished. The violence must stop!

Counselor

Abusing any human being is enough to make me weep . . . .

§

One thing that has made me weep and hurt my heart is to see someone abuse our elders. It is hard to imagine that people are not taught at an early age that these individuals are to be respected at all times. I was born and raised in the South, and we were taught that respecting our elders was as important as brushing your teeth in the morning. If you wanted to have a functional mouth—that is, lips that were not swollen and all 32 of your teeth still attached to your gums—the operative words to elders were "Yes, Ma'am," "Yes, Sir," No, Ma'am," "No, Sir," "Good morning," "Good afternoon," and "Good night." If you were asked to do something for your elders, you were expected to do it quick, fast, and in a hurry. Calling your elders by their first name would be considered a death sentence. There were certain rules concerning your elders, and you would adhere to those rules.

I worked in a nursing home when I first moved to Virginia. I was shocked and appalled by the blatant disrespect and ugliness that was directed toward some of the elders living in the nursing home. I was even more disgusted at the way some of the employees treated the elderly who requested something as simple as ketchup or more iced tea. The employees made comments like, "She doesn't need any more tea" or "He already had one pack of ketchup." Wow! Suppose that was your mother or father and someone refused them such a simple request?

I was also saddened by the way the young employees called the elderly by their first names. They said things like, "John doesn't do that." "Mary, do you need to go to the bathroom?" or "Sarah, please be quiet." These are people old enough to be their grandparents. There is a thing called respect. I have had elderly people call me nigger, and I still haven't disrespected them by calling them by their first names.

One employee was fired for pinching a 95-year-old lady. That is horrendous. Why would you work at a nursing home if you do not have the patience to care for these precious individuals? That is the objective of working with the elderly—to care for them. Some of these people do not have family, so the employees are their only family.

I think people have a tendency to forget that they, too, will grow older and may have to live in a nursing home. Remember—you reap what you sow. Seeing people not respecting the elderly and abusing them is enough to make anyone weep.

Alfreada Brown-Kelly

§

I am a Black woman who is attractive. I am smart and I was married for 20 years. I decided one day I would become the person God intended me to be, and I would seek God with all my heart. My husband was a Jehovah's Witness, and he did not approve of me because I did not accept his beliefs. He forbade my daughter to attend church with me, which was an attempt to discourage me from seeking my God, who is the Lord of my life. My husband caused all kind of trouble between me and my 12-year-old daughter. He told her not to attend church with me and took her places with him all the time, so she could bond with him and not spend time with me. One night, he and my daughter came home late, and he started complaining about the way I cleaned the house. He told many lies about me, and he told me to leave the house and he would raise my daughter. I did leave the house and I moved in with my parents.

Anonymous

Even though the devil tells you to destroy my will

The Holy Spirit continues to build

Makes me strong and instill in me His commands

That Jesus presents us with and demands

If I do His will and don't grow weary

If I faint not and refuse to become teary

Believe what He says is the truth

Walk in the light and not in the dark

The enemy will have no place in my world

§

I have cried often in my life. Like so many women, I have been abused and I have been hurt. I have experienced a broken heart. I have made poor choices and some horrid mistakes. I have gone through life giving nothing of myself, and I have gone through life giving so much that I just depleted myself. I have married at a young age for the wrong reasons and divorced for all the right ones. Yes, I have cried many times over the years. I have hollered to God above for something better in life. I have screamed to Him for the one thing I have always wanted—true love. I remember falling to the bathroom floor with my heart sitting in my stomach and my head tilted to heaven. "God," I said, "There has to be more to life than this. There has to be real love on earth. There must be a man that can love me for me." And then the moment came in my life when he answered my plea.

They always say that true love comes to those who wait for it. God put me in a place in which I had to learn to wait. For two years after my divorce, it was me and God. He sustained me, encouraged me, lifted me, and I kept going. He taught me and He prepared me. And then the day came when the waiting was over. I still cannot really understand how it happened. My mind cannot comprehend the mountains that had to be moved for love to occur. I remember the day with an unparalleled level of vividness. I remember the day true love rung my doorbell and stepped into my foyer. The moment I saw him, my spirit leaped. I knew that this was the one—the man who God sent to answer my plea. This beautiful man at my door was a single dad dropping his daughter off at my home for a sleepover. I had never seen him before, but when he came to the door to introduce himself, it was as if I had known him all of my life.

I later discovered that this man lived less than three minutes from my home, and I was puzzled by the fact that we did not cross paths sooner. I now understand that God holds everything in His hands, even time. God knew the hurt in my heart, and He knew it took time to heal my heart. God would not let love come into my life until He knew I was ready to receive it. I met my husband March 8, 2008, and we were married August 30, 2008.

So now, after all of the hurt, after all of the pain, after all of the feelings of worthlessness, and after all of the tears of despair—I weep. I weep every morning that I roll over and see my husband's face. I weep every time he holds me and every time he tells me how much he loves me. I weep every day he comes home from work and looks at me with a smile and every instance he holds my hand. I weep every blessed moment I kiss his cheek and his lips and whisper, "I love you" in his ear. I weep because every second that I look at my husband, I am reminded of my Heavenly Father's love for me. I know beyond a shadow of a doubt that I am honorable and precious to God, and He truly has a perfect plan for my life. I weep because now I truly believe that I am a queen, living on earth with my king, as we both live in honor of our King. This woman is full, this woman is complete, and this woman truly weeps.

Danita Brown

Time Stood Still

The first time I saw you
Our eyes locked
Time stood still

Your eyes penetrated my soul
Commanded me to follow
I followed
Time stood still

You touched my hand
Caressed my face
I trembled
Time stood still

You led me into a paradise
I was mesmerized
You kissed my lips
Time stood still

I was weak
You embraced me lovingly
Our hearts beat as one
And
Time stood still.

§

A woman cries when she reads a letter from another woman addressed to the man she thought was the love of her life saying how good it was being in bed with him, referring to her husband.

Lesson learned:

True love only comes from God, and never put your trust in man.

A woman cries tears of joy when her son graduates from high school and college with honors after she refused to let the educational system put the special education label on her child.

Lesson learned:

Always believe who God says you are and know that with Him nothing is impossible.

A woman cries as she watches her daughter endure social isolation and other problems because she is paralyzed, and the woman knows there is nothing she can do except to take God at His word—He will turn your mourning into dancing. He sent His Word and healed her, and by Jesus' stripes, she is healed. Her latter life will be better than her former.

Lesson learned:

God is in control . . . His Word will not return to Him void and that we shall reap if we faint not.

TL

LET GOD TAKE CONTROL

Sometimes we reach

into the depths of our souls

In order to take control

Of the ups and downs

that turns life around

grab hold of God's unchanging hands

believe He will sustain you

through daily pressures

and our best attempt to measure

The depth and width of His promises

His word a truth that continuously delivers us

Reach into the depth of your soul

And allow the Master to take total control

§

My son was two-years-old one December 16th when I came home from work to find that he had developed a fever and spots. According to the doctor, my son didn't have any of the usual childhood diseases, but the doctor didn't know what was wrong. We were instructed to do this, do that, do the other thing, and call if my son didn't get better. We called, went back, called again, spent an interminable Christmas Eve in the emergency room waiting for the staff of various departments to emerge from their holiday parties, and we were sent home again. By this time, all of his joints were swollen. He couldn't eat and he still had a fever, but the spots were gone. He spent the month of January in the ICU of a teaching hospital, much of the time on a refrigerated blanket that made him ache even more. I had to take an extended leave from my job to go to the hospital every day. But I went home every night because I was a single parent with two older children, and one of them was having frequent asthma attacks. My child had attacks only at night, though, so I took her to a closer emergency room on those nights. I didn't sleep much.

None of this made me cry. I occasionally trembled with worry. I trembled with anger when the doctor on rounds manipulated my son's joints to show the students how much it hurt him, but I didn't cry. I took one step at a time, was enormously grateful for the support of my wonderfully calm and retired parents, and tried not to look too far ahead.

What made me cry was my father's visit to the hospital. I never expected him to come because he tended to pass out in hospitals. I knew his mother had died in a hospital in the days when people in the country only went to hospitals as a last resort, and he visited her there when he was 11. He was such a strong man, with many household skills, an unshakable commitment to doing what was right, a beautiful singing voice reserved for Spirituals, great dignity, and a quiet love for his family. I adored him. Hospitals were his one weakness, so having him show up was a shock. He greeted me quietly and talked to my son a few minutes. I understood why he came, but I didn't say anything. He had come to say good-bye to his grandson, just in case. I hope I hugged him as he was leaving, but I honestly don't remember. He wasn't much of a hugger. That's when I cried.

My son was released from the hospital on February 28th. The doctors still didn't know what was wrong with him. He still had a fever but he was released. I gave him fever reducers every two hours around the clock, even when I was back at work. I fed him milk, cheese, and hardboiled eggs—all he could tolerate—and watched as he grew strong enough to walk again. A month later, his fever was gone, which was only by the grace of the Creator. My heart was full of thanks, and for this reason, I cried again.

Anita Harrell

Weeping, weeping, weeping

§

It has been stated, "No weapon formed against me shall prosper for I am more than a conqueror through Christ Jesus." This statement expresses how I felt until September 15, 2008. In my last semester of nursing school, I was hit with all sorts of weapons . . . from having my car towed twice, having to move out of my apartment and not knowing where I was going to stay, being low on money from time to time, and finding out that I may not graduate because of one class. Through all of this, I was still trying to stay focused on my studies. Every day it felt like another weapon was being thrown in my direction to the point where I just broke down crying. I wanted to give up.

Near the end of September until November, things slowly began to come together. I was able to pay the towing company to get my car back, move on campus, and have money in my pocket from my parents. There was still one weapon that I was dealing with—whether or not I was going to graduate. I prayed and prayed like Paul when he had that thorn stuck in him. I prayed and cried, prayed and cried. I stopped seeing the light at the end of the tunnel, but I still prayed and cried.

The evening of December 7, 2008, God spoke to me and said, "Stop worrying about your problems, for you should know that my grace is made sufficient unto you." On December 8, 2008, my professor asked to see me in her office. When she told me that I would be graduating, I didn't know what to do. I left her office, called my mom, and started crying, but instead of crying tears of sorrow, I was crying tears of joy! From these experiences, I have grown in my faith. I know that God is building me up and telling me to trust in Him for He'll never leave me nor forsake me.

THE ANSWERS

Sometimes there is confusion in our minds
No matter how we try to find
The answers to life's ups and downs
There is no answer to be found

So we search diligently and constantly
To find answers that is consistent,
accurate, practical and factual
Answers that have not been found

Stop and think about a man
That has all the answers and truly understands
That without Him we would be lost
That all the answers we find would be false

But if we lean on Him and depend on Him
All of the answers will be true
Because of His unconditional love
We will be able to get through
All of life's ups and downs

§

I cry when I see millions and millions of people taking God for granted. People don't realize that in some countries people cannot praise God openly and freely and must hide their Bibles. Religion is a freedom that Americans take for granted. It makes me weep when I see people continue to live in sin and make excuses for their actions. Many of them know the way but refuse to adhere to the Word of God.

I thank God that I am under the leadership and instruction of a great man of God who takes pride in ensuring that his congregation is taught God's principles and promises. For this I am grateful, and because of this, I am blessed. I thank God every day for saving me. Unlike human love, God's love is unconditional. And most of all, His grace and mercy endures forever.

Alfreada Brown-Kelly

WE TAKE FOR GRANTED

We take for granted

The man of God

We take for granted

The blessings of God

We take for granted

Our many healings

We take for granted

The way He directs us

We take for granted

His wondrous works

We take for granted

His love from above

We take and take

And take and take

And that my friends

Is our mistake

§

I weep for all the times I believed in one man who said that everything would be okay. I weep when the same man, who said he was my friend and lover, turned his back on me. It is hard to trust anyone these days, but then you can't hold the world responsible for your bad judgment. I met this man and fell in love without reading the signs: (1) When I called, he never picked up the phone; (2) After a few months of living together, I still didn't know his family; (3) He always had a reason why he couldn't be home for the holidays, even though he was not in the military. One day, I saw him in the mall Christmas shopping with another woman. So ladies, take my advice. Don't trust with blinders on and open your eyes. Also, don't be unfair and judge the next man because another man lied to you. God will put the right person in your path once you love yourself.

I WISHED I WAS ENOUGH

I wished I was enough
Even though I am smart and beautiful
I am not enough for you.

I wished I was enough
Even though I love the Lord with all my heart, all my soul,
and my entire mind
I am not enough for you.

I wished I was enough
Even though I had your children, cooked your meals, and
washed your clothes
I am not enough for you.

I wished I was enough
Even though I am humble, compassionate, and gregarious
I am not enough for you.

I wished I was enough
I am successful, educated, and talented
I used to wish . . . .

I was enough for you.

§

A time I cried was when I walked into my mom's room, and my mom was crying. She had been having a hard time remembering things, and she was upset and crying because she could not remember how to drive to her painting class that she had been going to for the last 20 years. I cried after I left her room because I realized that her memory problem was a real issue, not just ordinary forgetfulness. I had her tested shortly after that and she is currently being treated with Aricept, which is supposed to help people retain their memories, and it's used for Alzheimer's patients. I was really upset because I felt so bad for her. All I could do was hug her and tell her everything was going to be all right. I told her, "You are okay, just a little forgetful." I felt so bad for her because I knew she had a problem, but there was nothing I could really do about it except try and get her some help, which I did. I told her forgetfulness happens to all of us, and I tried to make the situation lighter for her. Although she now takes medication, losing her memory still really upsets her.

DP

MY MOTHER

As I watch this woman

Who is responsible for my existence

I smile to myself

I will be her one day

Her memory is not as strong as it used to be

This is a gentle reminder to me

I forget sometimes and I am younger than she

We laugh and talk about

Family members and yesteryear

Holding close in our heart

Memories that are dear

I watch my mother sit in her favorite chair

And thank God for her because she is the reason I am here.

§

When Mrs. Kelly first approached me about writing a book about women weeping and asked me to tell her about an incident that made me weep, I had the thought this was going to be a really sad, weepy book. However, over the last two weeks as I have thought about what has made me weep, I have realized that my weeping has been related to my joy and blessings. On Sunday, November 23, 2008, at St. John's Episcopal Church, our closing hymn for the morning service was "Amazing Grace." Understand, Episcopalians have been labeled as "the frozen chosen," as we don't display a lot of outward emotion in our public worship services. However, for me, this hymn has often elicited weeping. The first verse doesn't bring out the tears, maybe because I have been a Christian for a long time and accepted Christ as my Savior at a very young age. So, that Sunday, I made it through the first verse sans weeping. During the second verse, the weeping started. I think the emotion came from singing about and reflecting on how Christ has seen me through so many of the hard times (verse 2), has promised to be with me to the end of this life (verse 3), and how I will spend eternity with Him (verse 4). This song makes me feel really blessed and hopeful.

Amazing Grace, how sweet the sound,

That saved a wretch like me . . . .

I once was lost but now am found,

Was blind, but now, I see.

Through many dangers, toils and snares . . .

we have already come.

T'was Grace that brought us safe thus far . . .

and Grace will lead us home.

The Lord has promised good to me . . .

His Word my hope secures.

He will my shield and portion be . . .

as long as life endures.

When we've been here ten thousand years . . .

bright shining as the sun.

We've no less days to sing God's praise . . .

then when we've first begun.

Last Sunday, November 30, 2008, my husband gave me a beautiful birthday card (one day early) for my 60th birthday. We were celebrating the day with our grown children. The card stated how he wished he could give me luxuries and all the material things I might desire, but it said what he was offering was all of his love and devotion. The card was so touching that I asked him to read it aloud to me and my daughter, son, daughter-in-law, and son-in-law, so we all could hear how beautiful it was. Before my husband finished reading the card, all six of us were weeping. I again realized that weeping is an emotion, and often an emotion of joy and thankfulness . . . and I have much for which to be thankful.

Dr. Jane Mosshart Krumlauf

LORD GOD WHAT CAN I DO?

Lord God, what can I do?
That would please you and only you.

Sing a song?

Recite a love poem?

Read bible verses

From the book of Psalms?

Pray every day . . . .

Knowing that only you

Will make a way

I find delight in your peace

Knowing that only you

Can keep me in perfect peace.

Lord God, what can I do?
That will please you and only you.

§

There comes a time in a woman's life in which she has wept, whether it is because of sadness, happiness, tragedy, death, or a job. In the 18 years of my life, there have been few events that have caused me to shed a tear, with the exception of my grandmother's death in January of 2003. Cancer had embraced her for many years, but it finally took her during my seventh-grade year.

I still remember the last words I said to her, "See you later, Grandmommy," not knowing that "later" meant at her wake. It's amazing, really, that during the entire time leading up to her wake and funeral, I only shed a few tears. I was still in denial, her death not really hitting me. Now, as I reminisce about the times we shared, my tears seem to overflow, because I know she is gone and all I have now are memories. I still remember her helping me make crafts like my kindergarten bird project and paper airplanes. She was the first person to introduce me to reading classic children's books, and now I read all the time. We used to go on walks, and after each walk, I would come back knowing and learning so much more than before we left. My grandmother was consistently teaching and helping me grow, and she was the type of person who always put others before herself, even if and when it was an inconvenience.

I sit and think of all those years my grandmother was in pain, but yet she did not complain, not once. She continued to move on with life, even when life was trying to move away from her. Sometimes, without warning, I find myself crying or tearing up every time I think of her. Her death hits me harder now than at the time she died. She was 84-years-old, but I still feel like she was taken before her time. My grandmother was a strong and inspirational woman, and cancer took her away from me.

Her body is gone, but her presence and spirit are always with me. It's funny, but she is still teaching me from beyond the grave. She has taught me how not to take the little things for granted, to always try to put others first, and so much more. I was blessed to have had her as my grandmother, and all that she did for me will help me continue to grow.

Alicia Nicole Lewis

YOUR ANGEL

Sometimes in your life

God will send someone

To give you a word

So His will can be done

That someone

Will be strong

Encourage everyone to get along

Differentiate between right and wrong

Sing a praise song

That someone

Will have a heart of gold

A spirit that is bold

A compassionate soul

A superhero role

That someone

Will love all races

Judge fairly in all cases

Knowledgeable and spiritual

On a continuous basis

That someone

Will be your angel

§

I met my husband in May 1993 at a cookout, and we began a friendship that obviously developed into something much more. He was dealing with some relationship issues. I stuck by him, which seemed to solidify our friendship.

I noticed one of the most endearing qualities about my husband one day when we were riding, and a man was pushing his car in the street. It pained my husband not to be able to stop and help him. Another important quality about my husband is that he epitomizes the statement that the way a man treats his mother is a good indicator of how he will treat his wife. While we were still in the long telephone conversation stage of the relationship, I overheard his mother say some very harsh words to him and his only response was, "Yes, Mom. Yes, Mom." Now don't get me wrong, Mr. King can be rather callous toward his mother, as well as to me on some occasions, but I do know that he always puts the best interests of his family before his own personal wants or needs, and he is a very generous person.

While dating, I became pregnant with our son. Did this event happen in order? No, but I have never done things in the right order. God has blessed me with two healthy children. On Valentine's Day in 1994 while I was pregnant, we went to a local department store where I was told to pick out the ring I wanted. I guess that was his proposal. We planned our wedding date for July 15, 1995.

You have to take into consideration that I did not have my family in the area, and I was determined that this would be my wedding, not my mother-in-law's or anyone else's. I proceeded with my wedding plans that included dragging Mr. King to pick out colors for the wedding, invitations, food for the reception, and other things that he felt I should handle by myself or with a girlfriend. I immediately told him that this was our wedding, and he needed to be involved in the decision-making process.

The evening before our big day finally arrived. While on his way out of the house to go to his bachelor party, my husband asked me to give him the marriage license so he could give it to the best man for safekeeping. I trusted my husband to keep up with the license, but I did not trust his best man.

We all arrived at the church and were ready to begin the wedding march when someone came and told us that the pastor requested the marriage license. My face fell and I began crying because I realized that I had the license at my house, which was at least 15 miles away from the church. The traffic on I-64 was horrible on our wedding day. Luckily, my sister, who was not attending the wedding because she is a Jehovah's Witness, located the license at my house and eventually brought it to the church. My tears of joy and relief came during the wedding ceremony while my husband and I exchanged vows that we continue to uphold to this day. The tears of joy and gratefulness continued as I collapsed in my sister's arms, thanking her for saving my wedding.

PARADISE: INSIDE YOUR ARMS

There is a place I go
Called paradise
And in this place
I find solace and peace,
Understanding and love
Inside your arms.

There is a place I go
Called paradise
And in this place
I find respect and care,
Patience and kindness
Inside your arms.

There is a place I go
Called paradise
And in this place
I am never confused
Torn down or abused
And this place is
Inside your arms.

§

I have wept in times of difficulty when my children were in bad situations, and I knew I had taught them better. Feelings of disappointment and just not knowing where to turn have also caused me to weep. But I thank God for His Word and the people in my life who know and serve God. I have wept when I have felt lonely and not had someone to hold me and tell me everything was going to be alright. I have wept when I lost the man in my life who loved me and understood me when no one else did. I have wept when I realized that God was with me through all of these challenges, and He was there all those times I was disappointed, lonely, and afraid.

I SURVIVED

I survived

Through thick and thin

And all the chaos

In between

It was by His grace

The idea . . . .

I could see His face

In the special place

You know

On the throne

In His heavenly home

In that place called heaven

Streets filled with gold

Angels walking tall

Talking to God

I survived

The unexplained

All the crazy games

I survived.

§

As I sat at my youngest child's college graduation, I began to reflect on the journey that brought my family to this moment. I have wanted to put this story in writing for a long time and now the opportunity has come. I am the mother of two children, both born healthy with no obvious physical problems. Both children were later diagnosed with a hearing deficit that required hearing aids.

The youngest had a hearing deficit that had the most dramatic impact. His verbal skills were not developing as expected. Of course, the pediatrician believed that I was comparing my two children's developmental skills, and I was overreacting. As a mother, I felt it in my gut that something was wrong with my child's development, and I took it upon myself to have my son evaluated by specialists. One psychologist's test revealed some mental retardation, which was unacceptable to me, as well as a learning disability. The audiologist's test revealed that my son was hearing very little, and the audiologist wanted to put him in the hospital to do further studies to determine his brain wave activity. Although I considered doing this, I instead opted for a second choice and had my child evaluated by an ear, nose, and throat specialist. This specialist immediately put my child in the hospital and inserted pediatric tubes. The physician determined that there was a blockage in both ears caused by fluid. The experience in the hospital was traumatic for my son, but in three days he was trying to make sounds.

I placed my son in a private kindergarten to help with his transition from home. The teacher recognized he was having difficulty with learning sight words, numbers, shapes, and colors and recommended developmental evaluations. For approximately three years, I tried working with my son and the specialists to identify his type of learning disability. My son was angry a lot because he could not express his needs to anyone other than his sibling, grandmother, and me because people could not understand his method of communicating.

One night after putting him to bed, I had this urge to cry. At that point, I cried out to God for help. I cried to God that I was tired and did not know what to do to help my child. I heard God say to me, "I am in control." At that moment, I let go, let God, and my son started progressing. A sixth specialist, whom my son needed to help him progress, remained in his life until he accomplished the identified tasks.

The story does not end there because we had difficult years ahead with ear infections, visual changes, and multiple hospitalizations for respiratory problems. As a family, we dealt with each issue, and the bond between the siblings grew stronger. As a parent, I had to constantly remind myself that although my youngest child had a learning disability, I could not allow this to influence my expectations of him. As we took this journey together, I watched this child develop and cope with his adversities. He learned to adapt and move forward to achieve his goals. I have to admit most of the time I did not understand how he processed information. I watched as my son's learning disability gap of seven years decreased, and by the time he graduated from high school, the gap was closed. He can learn, but he just processes information differently.

The experience of raising a child with a cognitive disability has had a profound effect on my relationship with God. I watched God perform miracles all the time with my son. I learned and I still am learning to stand on His Word as I continue to learn how to let God into my life. I no longer ask why a situation is happening to me. I ask, "What lesson am I supposed to learn?" If I weep now, it is because I do not allow God to guide my footsteps.

LIMITATIONS

FOR US

BY US

FOR THOSE WHO ACHIEVE

THERE ARE NO LIMITATIONS

WE DON'T SET ANY!

§

At first, I was going to start at the beginning and talk about how my husband and I met, but I changed my mind. I will start near the end of our relationship. About two or three weeks before my husband left, we had our very first falling out. The issue was he put another woman before me and our marriage. I told him he had to choose between me and her, and his answer was he didn't want to choose. We tried talking it out, but this just made it worse. He started throwing all kinds of other issues in my face, comparing me to his "ex" and telling me what his coworkers were saying about me even if it wasn't true. When he wasn't with me, he was out partying, not truly understanding how lupus was wearing me out. He spent a lot of time just complaining.

Whatever the issue was that bothered him, he never brought it to light at the time it happened. He let things build up to the point where there was no changing his mind about leaving. I'm not saying that I was perfect, but I did admit to my wrongs in the marriage. I know I shouldn't have kept throwing it in his face about what he did, but I wanted him to hurt as much as I was hurting. I changed his cell phone number. Did it work? No. My husband was still talking to this other woman. I was hoping we could get past this problem, but to my surprise, we could not. On June 27, 2006, my husband left me with no money, no health insurance, and no food in the house. All of the things he put me through hurt me to my heart. I felt betrayed, less of a woman, not loved, heartbroken, lonely, depressed, and worthless. After he was gone for a week, I found out that he had the woman and her kids with him.

Two days before he left, I gave my life to God and was baptized in his name. Even though my marriage was going downhill, I still didn't give up on God. God allowed me to see that my husband wasn't the man I once loved. I wrote in my journals day in and day out and cried to everyone on the phone, except the person I should have been crying to—God. When I finally called out to God, blessings started pouring forth. I was able to stay in the house we shared with my kids; I was blessed to get a car of my own and a job. The lesson I learned is that regardless of what you are going through in life with marriage, children, finances, illnesses, etc., God is always there. If I don't know much else, I know I serve an awesome God. God said He would never leave me or forsake me.

For the two and a half years I was separated from my soon-to-be ex-husband, I thought I would never love again. I felt as if there was no one else out there for me. I was dating but I got tired of settling for less, and I wanted someone who loved and feared God like me. I wanted someone to love me for me, not for what I could do for him. I wanted to be treated like the queen that I am, and I could treat that someone like a king. I wanted 100% of a person. I wanted respect, honesty, faithfulness, love, understanding, and someone to make me laugh and accept me for not being a size 12. What I've learned the most is to have God as the driver and not as a backseat passenger, regardless of what I am going through in my trials, tribulations, and storms.

THE PRAYER

Father in heaven
I have been damaged
I still praise your name
My self-esteem is low
I still praise your name
My family has betrayed me
I still praise your name
My faith is shaky
I still praise your name
My anger is at a boiling point
I still praise your name
My hope is hopeless
But-I still praise your name

God,
Thank you for not giving up on me
Even though I do so quite frequently
God I thank you for being the awesome, true, and living God, prince
of peace, mighty healer and deliverer, that is always on time and never
late and whose mercy endures forever. I thank you, praise you, and
glorify your wonderful, marvelous and magnificent name.
Amen

§

An incident that has made me cry was the separation of my mother and me. As a young child, I never understood why I always thought she did not love me like my friends' mothers loved them. As I grew older, I learned to do without her, and I loved my grandmother as my mother. However, as a child I shut out my feelings about my mother, and rage and anger built up inside of me. When I did develop a relationship with her, we were never close. One day when I went to visit her, my cousin asked me several questions about missing my mom. It was at that moment that I broke down and cried. I finally realized it wasn't my mom's fault for the separation, and she left to protect both of us. My mom left me to protect my safety as well as to protect my feelings. When I realized this, I began to grow into the woman I am today. Now I am trying to save and restore my relationship with my mother.

§

In October of 2007, Mommy collapsed in the bathroom. I truly believed she was dead, and just as I was about to administer CPR, she came around. She walked out of the house with the fire rescue. She never remembered what happened. My sister flew down from Massachusetts, where she was going to school and working on her PhD. When I spoke to Mommy the night before she went to the hospital, I noticed that her speech was a little slurred and she said she was extremely tired.

When we arrived at the hospital, she looked like a wet dog. When I asked what was going on, the staff said she had a massive stroke that morning. The whole left side of her brain was destroyed, and the staff did not hold out much hope. She is still alive but she is nothing close to the person she used to be. She has no speech, is paralyzed on the right side, and is unable to do for herself. We put her in rehab for six weeks, and they all but kicked her out because she had no insurance and we couldn't get any assistance. I brought her to my house.

I had to put everything on hold to take care of her full-time. This was a definite challenge because we could only afford help for limited hours. All of her meds were $853 a month, and doctors' visits, therapy, medical supplies, and other expenses were out of pocket. So many doors were slammed in my face as I continued to fill out all kinds of applications for assistance. Mommy made the mistake of not becoming a citizen, and being a legal resident did not seem to count.

She did improve a lot and was able to feed herself. In February, she was hospitalized, and the doctors said there was nothing they could do. There were complications due to blood thinners that caused an intestinal bleed. This condition was further compounded by an allergy to aspirin. She came home, and I was getting her to stand up with a walker. In May, she went back to the hospital, and the doctors wanted to amputate both legs, but I refused. She did not improve and I could see death on her face.

They gave Mommy two weeks to live, and my house became her hospice with morphine and all. I refused to give it to her, and my sister and I decided to hold out on faith and take her home to the Bahamas against all professional advice. My sister and I bought her burial outfit and I got my Air Force uniform ready. We made the trip, one I never want to make again. She is still with us, and we are taking it one day at a time. Ayana and Len keep me motivated. God is good and I am truly blessed.

However, I lost my only grandmother 10 days after my mother became ill and a great aunt on Daddy's side two weeks later. I also lost my stepmother in April. In July, a family friend and her entire family were killed in an accident.

Peace
Hermionne (Emmy)

God said in his word: He will not put more on us that we can bear.

§

When I think of losing my loved ones, it makes me cry. I am very close to my family, and they are getting up there in years. I cry when I think of my life without them. What I do is think about how blessed I am to have them, and I try to enjoy their company while they are still here on earth. Time is precious and they are precious. I cherish my time with my family.

§

Why Women Weep

Why do women weep? Women weep when they are sad, mad, glad, and when they sense that they are about to walk into their destiny. When the labor pains of life are over and the miracle of life begins, this will bring forth tears of joy.

As for me, I will cry at the drop of a hat. Let me hear a testimony of how God turned what appeared to be an impossible situation into a blessing. Or better yet, let me begin to look back over my life and think of how good God has been and there I go—a waterfall.

I am known to weep when my friends and/or loved ones weep and rejoice when they are rejoicing. I weep when watching someone's life transform for the better: seeing a baby take his or her first steps; looking at a young man or woman walk across the stage to receive a diploma or degree; seeing a cancer patient healed and given another chance to live out his or her life; watching a single parent's dream of being a bride or groom become a reality; and seeing a homeless family move from a street, hotel, or apartment to a house. If I am allowed to witness a life changed and prayers answered, this will cause me to weep with undeniable joy and praise.

Now, don't get me wrong; I have had some tears of sadness because of a loss or disappointment, but the good that resulted is priceless. My tears bring forth hope and a promise from God, just as the rainbow did after the Great Flood. The important factor here is that it is all right to weep; weeping relieves stress, and I believe it allows us—in time—to move forward. The Word of God reminds us that we will have trials and tribulations but to be of good cheer and be encouraged because God knows our end like He knows our beginning.

My sister, you are stronger and better now that you have triumphed through the storm. Look in the mirror and see yourself as victorious. If you choose to look back, pull a sister or brother forward with an encouraging word or deed. Keep your eyes on the prize that is Christ Jesus. Stand tall and smile at your reflection. You are more than a conqueror; you are who God says you are! Now, if you must weep, do so knowing that weeping may endure for a night, but joy will come in the morning.

Marlene Johnson

Crying is a way of expressing ourselves.

§

Bible study is a beautiful place to be. It helps you get through a week that may have been stressful. But all in all, Bible study gives you hope to overcome obstacles that have tried to unsettle you and provides you with the opportunity to hear the Word of God. But what happens when the pastor throws you a curve ball and instructs you to do things that seem impossible, or, better yet, just plain crazy? Do you go with the Word of God or do you take matters into your own hands?

There was a time I would not only raise an eyebrow, but I would say openly, "I am not going to do that. Pastor must be clowning." Today, I weep tears of joy because I have learned I have to be obedient. Sometimes, I don't want to be obedient, BUT I HAVE TO BE! I have learned that when I do things my way, chaos occurs. I used to be the fixer. Today, I allow God to do his job: fix things. And when He fixes things, things that are done in the dark are brought to the light. And when you let God be God, Oh, my God! He turns things around, reminds you that no weapon formed against you shall prosper, and makes your enemies your footstool. Now, instead of weeping because I have botched a situation or thought I was "Mrs. Fix It," I let go and let God. I am weeping happy tears because I know when God fixes things they will never become broken again.

ABKelly

§

I weep today because I know God has brought me a mighty long way. I have lost family members who have been near and dear to me. I have been fooled and believed that relationships I were in were sacred, but they were not, and I have wasted many years trying to find myself. But in the last few years, I have been fortunate enough to be under the leadership of a great pastor, who not only teaches the Word of God, but also takes time to individually counsel his flock. I attend a church with a pretty large congregation with many assistant pastors, but the pastor of our church always makes himself available for his people. This is a very important thing to some people. True, assistant pastors are in place to aid the pastor, but when the pastor takes time to personally assist his flock, it means something to his congregation.

When my father died, I went to Louisiana for the funeral. Before I went to the church, I was informed that my pastor had called from Virginia to Louisiana, and talked to the pastor of my father's church and inquired if there was anything he could do to assist with the process. It made me feel so good to know that he cared enough about me to make that call. To some people, this act would mean very little, but to me it meant a lot.

I have learned from the pastor I have to pray for myself and talk to God. Just as my pastor prays for me and talks to God on my behalf, I have to learn to do these things on my own. What if the pastor is not there or is unavailable? Yes, I weep tears of happiness because I have finally learned that God listens to me in the same manner He listens to my pastor. I can pray the same way my pastor prays. And by doing these things for myself, I give my pastor time to attend to the needs of others in his congregation who have not grasped these concepts.

AB Kelly

I WILL DO HIS WILL

Although the Devil try to destroy my will

The Holy Spirit continues to build

Make me strong and instill in me His commands

That Jesus presents me with and demands

I do His will and don't grow weary

If I faint not and refuse to become teary

Believe what He says is the truth

Walk in the light and not in the dark

The enemy has no place in my world.

DOING HIS WILL

When you do His will

He will allow you to see

The indiscretions

And all of the transgressions

Your eyes will be open

Your ears will hear

Your heart will be receptive

Your mind will be clear

The enemy will flee

Because it's clear for all to see

When you do His will

He will set you free.

I used to try to figure out

Why you looked at me and scowled

Frowned at my accomplishments

Told the other women you hated me

And still pretended like I was your friend.

I used to try to figure out

Why your family disrespected me

Never accepted me

Downright rejected me

And put on a front in front of your friends.

§

On a luxurious spring day in 1970, I came home from a visit from Detroit, Michigan. As

I parked, I observed a scene that surely Rembrandt, Jacob Lawrence, or Michelangelo would

have envied and painted. My mother, with arms locked protectively around my nephew, sat in

an old-fashioned white rocking chair. As he cuddled his head under her chin, jealously shot from deep inside of me like fireworks in July (lament). I felt this wetness on my cheek (wail). I swallowed that emotion and tried to recall when I wept enough to get held in such a tenderly fashion as a child . . . somehow it all eluded me (whimper).

Now grown up, I find a rocking chair still emits a surprise cry (sob), weep, or sigh from me. I also remember my Mom's last days on that porch, rocking, smiling, sometimes wandering off, and our tears of joy when she'd be found. Tragically, her heart—so full of love, compassion, and caring for others—decided to take a rest (screams not tears). In 2000, the rocking chair that brought these memories was stilled and moved to its home with me (loud shout of pain). My fingers, which slowly and painfully configure these words, attempt to verbalize a pain that is unexplainable—even to other women who weep.

On the bright side, my brother just bought a farm and you guessed it, huh? Yep, there was a gray dingy, old rocker on the small porch of the house! Will he remember "Mom's rocker" and blubber or shed a tear? I truly hope so. It took six hours to sand, paint, cry, and rejoice at the finished white rocking chair being renewed in Mom's honor.

JM

TWENTY-ONE

I remember bleak St. Louis;
eight-and-a-half months on my birthday;
looked like a Volkswagen
in a city I never met before.
The third floor walkup was where we went,
thrown out of the country place
because of the German Shepherd—my Christmas gift.
Gas jets stuck from walls;
grease-black oven made me cry;
the dog chased mice each morning
till I was through vomiting,
dressed, took it out
downstairs, across the street, to the park,
to finish in rain
what it started in the shower stall.
Fridays, he came home
past midnight; how did he drive?
Sundays, downtown together,
lingered, shivering, by a shop-window mink,
hurried past the bar—his name? Woman's voice?
I remember the envelope:
plane ticket, Mama's careful hand:
"Come home to have the baby."

Patsy Anne Bickerstaff

§

Why do women weep? Wow! That's a discussion question that could go on for days at a time. We, as women, have many different stories to tell and that's what makes us unique. I question myself as to how the words would flow in writing this journal entry, but as they say, "It is what it is."

I have been through many rough patches in my life. One way or another, I have seen the light at the end of the tunnel to get me through these times . . . with God's help. I remarried about five years ago, thinking this time around I was going to do things differently. I was going to make sure that I addressed any issue with my husband before we got married, so we started with a clean slate . . . not!

I want to say this before I begin to tell you my story. I loved my husband 110%. The problem was he, like other men, didn't appreciate what he had nor was he satisfied with just one woman. I was going to move myself and four children out of state because my husband finished school and received an offer for a better job. I guess you are thinking, "Great! What's wrong with that?" Nothing, but I didn't think the timing was right. First of all, I had just found out that I was four months pregnant with our second child. Okay, I want to take a two-second pause from the move for a moment and let you know that I had two children before I met my husband. I was done having children, but my husband did not have any children (insert joke here!), biological children, that is.

Well, anyway, I had my tubes untied so that I could conceive children with my husband. I wanted this too, so don't get me wrong. I love my two children with my husband more than life itself. There is nothing I wouldn't do for them; but let's be real, I was done having babies. So that being said, we were going to move out of state. I left my house that we built from the ground up, which was brand new, and all of my family for a better life . . . so I thought.

My husband relocated four months ahead of me while I was left to sell our home and raise the children by myself. Oh, yeah, did I mention I was pregnant—eight months to be exact—and still working? So, while I'm home holding down the home front, my lovely husband was out of state having what he called "movie night" with a mutual friend of ours with her and her four kids. Oh, yeah, did I mention the friend's mother was there as well? Yes, ladies, he was having "movie night" with another lady, her kids, and the mother . . . I guess this was his surrogate family away from home.

This lady was doing everything that I guess I would have been doing if I was there with my husband, including sleeping with him in my damn house. Okay, can you say I was beyond pissed when all of this came to a head? This man I loved soooo much just gambled his family away for a piece of ass. I'm bitter—hell, yes!

I gave up everything for this man and put my family first. There was nothing I wouldn't do for my husband, and this just hit me like an Amtrak train. I woke up every morning feeling like someone had hit me with a car. I cried every day for months I was so depressed. I just couldn't get over the pain that I felt, and nothing could help me escape it.

I had to really hit rock bottom to come out on top in this horrible situation in which I was placed. I prayed every night and asked God to help me through this and He did. He said to me, "You have been through a lot, sister girl, and guess what? You're going to be a better person for it and much stronger because tomorrow is a new day and better things are coming your way." I've always said that if you continue to settle then you're blocking true blessings from coming into your life. I will never settle and be anyone's second choice. I should be a priority, not an option.

I guess I could go on for days with this story but the reality is this: I've been through another rough patch in the road, but that doesn't mean that I'm just going to sit back and feel sorry for myself. Oh, ladies, never that . . . One thing my Mama instilled in me is to hold my head high and demand respect for myself. I know that I'm going to be a better person for the journey that I've taken thus far and a far better woman at the new beginning that lies ahead for me.

SONYA P

A STATE OF CONFUSION

When your mind is confused

And Satan has control

You become disoriented

And don't know what is real

You live in a daze

And a state of confusion

And believe in your heart

Things that are really delusions

You are so far gone

Truth could stare you in face

It wouldn't make a difference

Because you're in a state of confusion.

§

Why Women Weep

Hmmmm . . . let me first reflect on my initial recollection of weeping. As a young girl, I can remember being whipped for disobedience. I cannot recall which rule I disobeyed; I just remember the pain of the whipping that made me vow to never do "it" again, whatever "it" was supposed to be. My best recollection of weeping occurs when reflecting on how and when God has showed up and showed out! So, as several songstresses have done in the past, I'll share a collection of my best hits.

In junior high school, I recall watching Mommy have a stroke right before my eyes. Observing this event was quite traumatic. Seeing her in the county hospital intensive care unit with several tubes and catheters in her was tearfully scary. If screaming and weeping out of fright is a form of a meltdown, then it was the first meltdown that I can recall experiencing. In the meantime, I will return to the urban county hospital scene. I always perceived my mother as a woman of strength, enthusiasm, goal orientation, and determination who was very opinionated and direct. Seeing her in the intensive care unit hospital bed with all of those tubes and catheters and not being able to respond to my presence was a first for me.

I remember being in the living room of Miss Clara's home at the time Mommy had the stroke, but I don't remember if we were living there at the time or just visiting for the day. I do not recall the details of the ambulance's arrival or my grandmother's arrival after a 24-hour bus ride to New York City from Florida. After making several more visits to the hospital and physical rehabilitation unit to see Mommy, Grandma Irilla took my sister (7-years-old) and me (14-years-old) back home with her. The events that followed had a strong impact on my values and career.

As children often do, we quickly adapted from an urban lifestyle to a suburban lifestyle. We performed excellently in school and learned how to do chores in and around the house, including raking the yard and attending to planted vegetables in the back. Mommy visited my sister and me at Grandma Irilla's home once she completed her physical therapy and could walk with a quad cane. Mommy weighed less than 100 pounds at the time. My sister and I were great hostesses during Mommy's visit. She enjoyed several meals with us and saw how well we were adapting academically. Education, learning, and teaching were her passions.

What my sister recalls most about relocating to Grandma Irilla's home is that Grandma gave up her one bedroom for us to sleep in and created a bedroom for herself on the back porch. Then, unexpectedly, one day my sister and I were all packed up and sent on a 24-hour bus ride back to Mommy in the big city. Mommy was not aware that we were on our way. Reflecting on what all could have happened, but did not happen by the grace of God showing up and showing out, I feel is enough to make a mature person tearful, let alone a 16-year-old girl and her 9-year-old sister.

In high school, I was excelling academically as most teens did. Once we moved into our own apartment, I remember working part-time as a dental receptionist on weekends and ensuring the comfort and safety of Mommy and my younger sister daily. I was kept quite busy; in fact, busy enough to remain out of trouble. It was God again showing up and showing out. You see, upon our return to the big city, my younger sister and I did not go directly to where my mother was staying because we did not know where she lived.

Instead, we went straight from the Greyhound bus station in Times Square to the home of one of her old co-workers who we kept in contact with while living in Florida with Grandma Irilla. Her name was Miss Mary Kay, and she was gracious in taking in both of us. She taught me two of her great Virginia family recipes that have stayed with me over the years, meat loaf and macaroni and cheese. This was my first exposure to spending "girly girl" time together with someone else besides my mother. It was fun learning more about cooking. I had a semester of cooking and sewing classes in junior high school while living with Grandma Irilla, but this was the first time I was supervised in the kitchen at home.

Miss Mary Kay re-enrolled us in the New York City school system. Once she realized there was a drawn-out process to getting public assistance for my sister and me, she rightfully took the shortcut and dropped us off at the downtown office of the Department of Social Services. Ironically, the person who Mommy was living with had dropped Mommy off at the Department of Social Services the same day. I remember that it was a sunny spring day of waiting, waiting, and waiting for our case to be heard and handled by a social worker. I believe the divine reunion with Mommy made the long hours of waiting our turn for housing and family assistance more tolerable. At four o'clock in the afternoon, a Department of Social Services staff member came to us in her most kind, cordial, and professional voice stating, "It is closing time and you must leave, but your homeless case will be one of the first ones heard and dealt with when the doors open in the morning at eight o'clock."

I was 16-years-old sitting on the sidewalk at 4:30 in the afternoon with my mother and sister, wondering where to use the bathroom, when a man passed by asking why a family was sitting on the ground outside of the Department of Social Services. When he heard how our day started and progressed, he asked us to follow him home. So you ask, "What was a school crossing guard doing walking home in the projects at 4:30 in the afternoon if school closes at 3:00?" I do not blame you; I often ask myself the same question. Since we defied all the rules of safety as ladies and girls by following a stranger, the response again is, "God shows up when you least expect."

The stranger was named Mr. JB, and he took us home with him and we met his wife and son. Mrs. JB prepared the most nutritious hot dinner, provided a cozy pull-out sofa bed for us
to sleep on that night, and made a full-course breakfast the next morning. As promised, with the assistance of Mrs. JB, we returned to the Department of Social Services at 8:00 in the morning. Due to the persistence of Mrs. JB, the community activist, we received whatever it took to go find, rent, and furnish an apartment. Incidentally, this apartment was next door from where one of our previous apartments had caught fire and burned down years earlier. There again, God showed up and out, giving Mommy the strength and perseverance while using a walker to accomplish what most people take for granted: finding and maintaining housing. Mommy even received help with homemaking assistant services, where we met Mrs. Elena Browne, a licensed practical nurse who was assigned to Mommy's case.

Reflecting back on the sequence of events, I have shed many happy tears about graduating from high school with a Regents diploma and attending a community college in spite of having no knowledge of how significant SAT scores were to getting into college. Nonetheless, the family tradition and meaning behind wearing all-white attire for graduations was instilled in my sister and me during my high school graduation. Mrs.

Elena Browne made a contribution to our family and to the profession of nursing by instructing me to select nursing as my major instead of early childhood education when I registered at the community college. God showed up and I obeyed. God showed out five years later, after several trials and tribulations, when I graduated from the community college with an associate's degree in nursing. Over the years, these trials developed my values and strengthened my character. Eventually, Mrs. Elena Browne assisted Mommy in moving to a downstairs apartment of a two family, private home to decrease Mommy's struggle with her unsteady gait as she was walking up and down the stairs.

In summation, I would like to focus on three major points. Point one is the importance of recognizing, avoiding, and handling meltdowns. Seeing my mother in the intensive care unit in a life-threatening condition after having a stroke was a defining moment for me and my relationship with God. I learned then that "God is your rock and resource; Get to know Him early in life and prevent your meltdowns in distressful times." As a critical care nurse who has this event frozen in my mind, I make it part of my practice to always prepare the family/visitors of critical patients as to what they can expect to see before they go over to their loved ones bedsides.

Point two is the importance of spending quality "girly girl" time with adolescents. The time Miss Mary Kay spent in nurturing my creative cooking skills and sharing her Virginia family recipes during my fragile teen years was priceless. Sharing cooking skills is not done often enough in homes these days; this practice has yielded to relying on fast food chains that determine our families' nutritional habits. My mother and grandmother did not know how to make time to pass down their skills. I recall my sewing skills were not nurtured at home while living with Grandma Irilla, despite her having excellent creative abilities and a sewing machine in the house. My grandmother hid her great sewing skills that she eventually took to the grave with her. I learned to value both cooking and sewing, and I share these skills with my children and protégés. In parenting skills programs, I passionately teach parents how to spend quality time with their children by doing things with them that they once enjoyed doing themselves. Teaching will help nurture their children's values and characters. For example, my daughter's love of science was nurtured from a young age, and now she is a medical student.

The third and last point is the importance I place on real estate investing. One may wonder why a professional registered nurse would value having extra property or space to share in the event strangers may benefit from having a leg up or boost, so to speak. Attentive reflection to pivotal events in my life gives me my response. Look at the many people who took my mother and her two daughters into their homes. Then, look at the many contributions to society and the nursing profession that I have been able to make as a result of this assistance. My values and character development helps one to understand why I show off for a God who shows up and shows out. I weep to praise God for positive outcomes, miracles of past and present, and His purpose and plans for my life.

Sunshine

§

There is nothing more hurtful than the day I found out my husband had betrayed our marriage vows. It was early on a Saturday morning and I was going to the hairdresser to get my hair done. I picked up the mail on the kitchen counter and my husband's phone bill was in the pile of mail. While at the hairdresser, I proceeded to go through the mail. Even though my name was not on his phone bill, I immediately got sick—I knew something was wrong.

As a woman, when you get the feeling something is wrong, something is wrong. I was wondering to myself, Why is this bill so thick? Well, the bill was thick because he had been calling one number two, three, four, five, six times a day. And one of the times he called the number was when he told me, and I quote, "When I get off from work, I like to listen to music to get my mind straight before I get home." When he told me that, I thought to myself, This sounds like a lie. But the real reason he was late was because he had to talk to her on his way home. If you are going to be a player, learn the playa rules. Why would you have an itemized bill sent to your house? Can you say it with me?—CRAZY!

I saw a number on my home phone a couple of times. I did not know the number, so I asked my husband and daughter if they knew who was calling. My husband declared he did not know who it was, and it must have been a wrong number. He blatantly lied every time I asked. And while he came home every night, he maintained a relationship with this woman who admitted to me years later that she had low self-esteem, and she wanted to believe he would one day leave me. To add injury to insult, the woman started calling my house and hanging up. I knew it was her and I told her, "Please come get your man (my husband)."

Then I started to remember the little things my husband used to tell me: "Everybody at my job is sleeping with someone else. The people there are so trifling, and all of the women are whores, dykes, lesbians, and gays." Well, he did say *everybody* was sleeping with someone else and that included him. This woman of little worth started calling my job. Years later, she would tell me she hoped I would just get tired of her harassing me, and I would just pack up and leave. I asked her, "If you participated with him in trying to hurt me, did you not think he would not hurt you one day?" Years later, this heifer called me crying and said, "We need to talk." I responded, "We, like in you and I? What are we going to talk about?" She said, "I am tired of your husband lying to me. He is never going to leave you." I said, "Duh!!!!!! Why would he? Let's compare facts. You have three kids by three different men. You have a GED. He met with your ex-husband, and he verified that you are a whore. You have little education, and you were stupid enough to believe that he would leave a woman of worth for your simple ass. But even if he did, you two deserve each other."

As for my husband, he still tried to play me. He told me I was reading too much into things. I cannot tell you how this situation impacted my life, but unlike most women who endure betrayal, I did not fall apart. I trusted God for guidance and excelled in more ways than one—for me to trust God and not get even on my own was a miracle in itself. God made my enemy my footstool. The other woman gave me proof of the affair, information that confirmed my suspicions, and told me more things than any one woman should have to handle. She opened my eyes to many things. I bet today she doesn't even know why she told me all the things she did. **But God**—can you say it with me—**But God said in His Word He would make your enemies your footstool.** Hallelujah!

I wept for her and the countless other women who waste so many years of their lives waiting for a married man to leave his wife. Have some class in your behind and tell that fool, "When you get a divorce, call me." As long as you are stupid enough to stay with him, he will have his cake and eat it too. Why would he leave his wife when you make yourself available at his beck and call? He has already told you he cannot spend any holidays with you, and he cannot stay the night with you. You can have whatever is left over that his family does not use. I then said, "You have daughters. What message are you conveying to them? Maybe one of the messages you are conveying is my mother is a whore who puts up with men who are married, so I will follow her footsteps."

Yeah, I wept. I wept because I was involved in this stupid, ignorant mess. I wept because I couldn't hurt them the way they hurt me. I wept because I had to be the bigger person and ask, "What Jesus would do?" Did I want to do what Jesus would do? No! I wanted to get even. Sometimes counseling helps. In my case, my husband wanted sympathy and empathy.

He broke our marriage vows, but he told me it was my fault. Pastors will tell you to pray and that you must forgive and forget, but do we ever forget this type of indiscretion? Your only hope is to pray, pray some more, and then pray some more. Pray that one day you will be able to let it go. But trust me, readers, you will never forget.

A Woman of Worth

HER

You had the audacity
To call my house
And ask for my husband
Like he was your spouse

You proceeded to tell me
My husband loved you
And you wished our marriage
Was not the truth

Because I am not
The person I used to be
I felt sorry for you
Because he is "my husband" you see

You gave away
Many years of your life
With a liar and a cheater
Who would never make you his wife

My Father in heaven
Forgive them both for what they have done to me
Continue to strengthen me
And set my mind free.

HIM

You strung her along
For many years
People wondered why
I looked like I didn't care

I knew in my heart
Something was wrong
I couldn't give 100%
All along

I often stepped back
And watched the expression on your face
As a result
As your wife, I couldn't take my rightful place

You lied, stole, and cheated
Gave away precious hours
With a worthless whore
Who had no power

You went to church every Sunday
Knowing you were doing wrong
But the Lord was nowhere in your heart
You couldn't even sing His songs

A woman knows
When something is not right
She has to continue to pray
With all of her might

What's done in the dark
Will come to the light
And the wife has to allow
Jesus to fight her fight.

§

Women, women, women! Weep, weep, weep! Why, why, why? Since the foundations of civilizations were built, women have played roles that have traditionally been called "women's roles" based on instinctive notions, cultural orientations, and sanctioned norms and values within the particular society in which a woman lives. What is a traditional role in one culture may be an anomaly within another culture. Women still have biological, psychological, sociocultural, and spiritual response sets to being placed in these defined roles, and these response sets constitute patterns revealing why as women we weep.

Women tend to weep out of joy, sorrow, ambivalence, or a combination of all three states. As I relate the following incident, please know that all three states have been experienced at different moments in time. We bathe in tears, but when we look beyond the cleansing from the tears, we find a pain that is likened to an itch not soothed by a scratch.

I lived with my parents next door to a family of four girls being reared by a single mother who was widowed several years earlier. I was two years older than the third daughter, but we all did everything together. All of the girls and I became close friends walking to school together, participating in church and Bible school, attending birthday parties, skating in the street, and playing four corners and baseball in the field near our home. We separated only when we grew up, and they started working and I went away to college. The oldest daughter got married and had three daughters. Each time I would come home, one of her daughters, Dionne, would run to me and plead with me to take her with me. She did not care where I was going. She wanted to go. Each time I left, I would leave her standing behind the screen door with tears streaming down her face as if she had lost her best friend. As she grew older, her behavior did not change. So, when I got married, I told her the next time I came home in the summer I would bring her to live with me in the northern city in which I resided at the time. That summer would be too late.

Dionne drowned in a lake during the church picnic. I was devastated when I received the call. I blamed myself for many years even though I believed it was not God's will for her to leave her family to move in with me. This incident happened over 30 years ago, and it has made me want to support many of the desires young people have for things and give them their needs and wants. Dionne is always with me, and I feel her love and remember the times we spent together. I have a granddaughter who is 10-months-old, and I think about Dionne as I look at my granddaughter and watch her precocious behavior. Sometimes when we are alone together, I weep. I do so because I want so much for her life, and I continually pray for her to be successful.

What caused me to weep then and to this day is the pain under the surface of a wound that looks healthy, but is still tender to the touch. The layers of tissue beneath the wound are still not healed. This incident occurred early in my young adult years during which the life of a young girl named Dionne became enmeshed with mine during my comings and goings in a small southern community that I called home. This sharing in Dionne's life impacted mine, and losing her caused me to weep because I knew she had experienced fear in the darkness of the cold lake as she drowned. I remembered our warm embraces and the thought of her being alone in the water until her lifeless body was pulled to shore haunted me. Later, I have come to know that she lives with me each day of my life.

As I have thought about this incident throughout the years, it has caused an awakening in my soul, one that guides me each day with an intense prompting to do something special for someone's child at each opportunity given and to seek opportunities as well. This awakening reminds me why God replaces weeping with action by stirring the brain to increase oxygen and blood flow. This stirring causes the physical body to act, and there is an intensity to respond to the physical action with spiritual action. I have learned that my spiritual walk includes an ability to recognize that the belly button sensation I often feel is in fact the stirring of the Holy Spirit.

Attempting to learn from experience is a right of every child of God. Having faith in Him does not exempt us from weeping in actuality or symbolically, and it does not exempt us from sorrow. He instructs us best in the following Scripture:

A time to give birth and a time to die; a time to plant, and a time to uproot what is planted. A time to kill, and a time to heal; a time to tear down, and a time to build up. A time to weep, and a time to laugh; A time to mourn, and a time to dance. A time to throw stones, and a time to gather stones; A time to embrace, and a time to shun embracing. A time to search, and a time to give up as lost; A time to keep, and a time to throw away. A time to tear apart, and a time to sew together; A time to be silent, and a time to speak. A time to love, and a time to hate; A time for war, and a time for peace." (Ecclesiastes 3:1-9, NKJV).

Jesus is moved when our Spirit is troubled. This is evident in the story of Lazarus's death when his sister Mary was weeping. This scene is instructive. As the Bible says, "When Jesus therefore saw her weeping, and the Jews who had come with her, also weeping, He was deeply moved in spirit, and was troubled, and said, 'Where have you laid him?' They said, 'Lord, Come and see.' Jesus wept. And so the Jews were saying, 'Behold how He loved Him!'" (John 11:33-36, NKVJ). Jesus taught in parables, and this story reminds us that we do not suffer alone. Even in our weeping, Jesus has compassion for us.

Dionne, although I want to feel your physical presence, I know now that you and I have been brought closer than I could have imagined. Your spirit is ever present and has been since you went to rest with Him. I am better for you having touched my life. Much love!

Marie

§

That Fateful Day

The date was January 11, 1987. I will never forget that day for as long as I live. That is the day that changed my life forever. Let me start from the beginning. My mom had me when she was 17 . . . her sperm donor, I think the term most children use is daddy, was never really a part of my life. Anyway, my mom enlisted in the United States Air Force when I was about one or so. She left me in North Carolina, and Grandma Alice and Aunt Mamie raised me. I lived with them until my mom came back to get me when I was eight. I can remember being four or five and telling Mamie, "My mommy's coming home this weekend, so I have to call her mommy, but when she leaves, I'll call you mommy again, okay?" Although she never said anything, I think that hurt her.

Fast forward to 1982. Aunt Mamie was diagnosed with breast cancer. She started chemotherapy and things were looking up for a while. I remember her losing her hair and it growing back like peach fuzz, each time more beautiful than the last. She was always so optimistic and never questioned God as to why this was happening to her. Even though I always stayed with Grandma Alice during the summer, in 1986 I stayed with Mamie. I wanted to be there for her in case she needed anything. I can remember one day in particular. I was in the guest bedroom and Mamie was in her room moaning (I think that she was always in more pain than she let on). All of a sudden, she was silent. I ran into the room to check on Mamie and do you know what she had the nerve to do? She looked at me and my cousin with a smile and said, "Y'all thought I was dead, huh?" Needless to say, I was not amused at all.

After school started in the fall, I saw Mamie on the weekends. I also spent Christmas break with her. Although I'm ashamed to say this, I yelled at her. She asked me to wash dishes and being the smart mouth 14-year-old that I was, I wanted to know why I had to clean a sink full of dishes that I didn't use. I left my grandma's house slamming the door. Later that night, my mom, stepfather, and I were at Mamie's house getting ready to head back to Virginia, and I told her that I was sorry and that I loved her. I also told her about a boy at my school whom I liked and asked her if I should tell him. That was January 4, 1987.

On Sunday, January 11, 1987, I was in the bathroom washing up because we were getting ready to go to UNC Chapel Hill Hospital to see Mamie. She had been hospitalized again during the previous week. I remember being excited because I had not seen her in a week, and as usual, I had so much to tell her. I heard the telephone ring while I was washing my face and then my mom saying, "She's gone." At that moment, I stopped washing up and slid down the wall to the floor crying and asking repeatedly, "Why did you leave me?" Although I knew Mamie was in heaven and no longer suffering, I missed her. I kept thinking, "I am so glad that I got a chance to apologize."

On January 11, 1987, I lost my second mother, my aunt, and my best friend. Mamie Huff was all of that and more to me. She died at the tender age of 33 . . . 27 days shy of turning 34. She was never married and did not have any children. Have you ever met someone everybody loved and no one had a bad thing to say about? Someone who always put others first and kept the family together? That was my Aunt Mamie. Although I knew that she was loved, I guess I didn't realize how much she was loved until I was at the funeral. There were so many people. I'm a country girl from Henrico, North Carolina, you see, and believe me when I say that I think the entire community showed up to pay their respects to the most beautiful woman that I have ever known inside or out. Mamie was so giving that although she died of breast and lung cancer she donated her organs to science. I don't know how many people would be thinking of others up until the end.

I still think about her all of the time, especially on January 11th, her death; January 14th, her funeral; and February 7th, her birthday. Some nights I just cry myself to sleep when I think about her and how she was gone too soon. Shoot, I'm crying now. Rest in peace, my beautiful angel, and remember that you will **ALWAYS** be loved.

P.S. If you are wondering if I ever told that boy I liked him, I did. We celebrated our 19th wedding anniversary on Valentine's Day this year.

Pamela F. Sutton

§

When asked to discuss a time when I cried, my mind immediately flooded with memories of deaths, births, graduations, heartache, fear, and so much more. However, one memory, one pivotal moment in my life, caused tears of joy to flow from my face. On December 30, 2007, my husband, Jermaine Ellis, proposed to me. This was a time of pure elation, but it is not the moment that caused me to weep. A week after Jermaine proposed to me, I scheduled an appointment with my matron of honor and bridesmaids to go look at dresses. Selecting a wedding dress can be a time of stress or a time of joy. My selection process was a moment that will stay with me forever.

Let me give you a little background. I was a single mother of one daughter, with a limited income, and my parents were in the middle of a bitter divorce. This was a time in my life where I was supposed to be so happy, but I was constantly battling mixed emotions. It is every girl's dream to have her parents provide both financial and emotional support for her wedding. Unfortunately, neither parent was available to me.

Imagine the emotional roller coaster of being happy one day and sad the next. How will I be able to afford a wedding? Who will be there to talk me through the process? While I was trying to figure everything out, God had already worked it out. As soon as I stepped into the bridal shop, my best friend—Joi Lewis—saw a picture of the dress I wanted. It was perfect. The dress fit like a glove, and I didn't want to take it off. I looked and felt like a beautiful queen. There was no question that this was the dress for me.

It was checkout time. I couldn't possibly pay for my dress on the same day, so I looked into layaway. In order to place my dress on layaway, I had to put 50% down. I reached for my check card, and my best friend and matron of honor, Joi, closed my wallet and paid for my dress in full. I cried. An overwhelming feeling came over me, and I couldn't stop crying. I didn't understand why she would do this for me. Someone whom I love so dearly extended a love so genuine and selfless to help make my day special.

To this day, I still cry tears of gratitude and appreciation, tears of hope, and tears of joy because of what my friend did for me. While I was looking for help from a traditional source, my parents, God revealed to me that He will supply all of my needs. That moment of sisterly love reminded me that I am loved. That random act of kindness penetrated my soul, and I will forever be grateful for Joi's generosity. This act may seem small to some, but God knew that this act would change my life forever. He knew exactly what I needed, provided it for me, and I cried.

Nicole Ellis

I Will Not Be The Afterthought

I will not be the afterthought

I need to be your first thought

Leftovers has never been my forte

Not to mention, a second place lady

Give to me your very best

And save for all the others

Whatever you have left

I deserve to be number one

If not to you,

Perhaps number one to

another

ACKNOWLEDGEMENTS

First of all, I thank my Lord and Savior, Jesus Christ, for all of the women who took time out of their daily schedules to assist me with this book. I had this idea in my head for a long time. Then I started to dream about it, talk about it, and I asked people, "What do you think about the idea?" I called my friends and mentors and asked their opinions. Then I called my mother and asked her what she thought. I called many of you who contributed to this book, and I received various responses. Some of you told me that you could write a book about weeping; others wanted to know if I would use their names. This book is not about us, but it is a tool to be used by others to let them know that life happens. The same things that have happened to us have also happened to others. As a result, we have all had to weep, but we have all overcome our struggles to become superior beings. We are stronger physically, emotionally, and spiritually.

To my daughter, Victoria, I love you with all my heart. Remember everything I tell you. I know not the day or hour my time on earth will end. My hope is that you will grow up to be a well-rounded individual who has principles and morals. I say to you, "Do unto others as you would have them do unto you."

To the Hampton University School of Nursing, I thank all of you for your continued support. To everyone who will read this book: life happens. Sometimes we will be on the bad end of the stick. Sometimes we will be the recipient of rewards. We must always pray and pray diligently. We must ask God for wisdom and understanding to sustain us. With Him, we can do and overcome all things. Without Him, we cannot survive. Choose to be a survivor.

Alfreada Brown-Kelly

In Memory

To all of the angels who have gone to heaven before me. I love all of you and a part of each one of you lives in my heart. I miss all of you.

Junius Reado

Victoria Butler Reado

Oliver Brown, Sr.

Norman Every, Sr.

Kenneth Louis Brown, Sr.

Clarence Brown, Sr.

Mary Elizabeth Kelly

Margie Hill

Janie Bassett

Terry Adams Williams

Alfreada Brown-Kelly: Biography

Alfreada Brown-Kelly is an author of poetry who lives in Hampton, Virginia. Alfreada is a native of Thibodaux, Louisiana and previously lived in New Orleans, Louisiana for ten years. Alfreada has been writing poetry for years and has started on a children's collection called the Victoria E. Kelly series. As a child, reading was her favorite hobby and the weekly highlight was waiting for the bookmobile to arrive to check out as many books as possible. Alfreada is a graduate of Nicholls State University and Old Dominion University. She is currently a graduate student at Old Dominion University in Norfolk, Virginia. She is an avid reader who enjoys reading poetry, biographies and Christian and contemporary fiction. *Transformation of The Mind, Body & Soul* is her first book. Her second book of poetry is *The Skin I Am In*. Alfreada's poetry has been featured annually in Ancestral Rites, a poetry anthology published by BookClubEtc, *Praise Magazine,* and Hampton Roads *My Time* magazine, (September 2010 and January 2009), *The New Journal & Guide Newspaper and Diversity Times* newspaper. For more information please visit her website at www. alfreadabrownkelly.com or email her at AlfreadaKelly@aol.com

Thanks to all the women who helped me to make this book a success. You all hold a very special place in my heart.

Dr. Lydia Figueroa

Mrs. Debra Owens

Dr. Melinda Barker

Mrs. Jennifer Bellanger

Ms. Carla F. Brown

Ms. Gleneice Hopson

Tonya

Dr. Melissa Gomes

Ms. Patricia Alston

Mrs. Holly Winston

Mrs. Angela Seward- Trabbold

CW

Mrs. Cassandra Brown Coney

Ms. Phyllis L. Jones

Ms. Hermanda Prioleau

Ms. Shyla Miles

Mrs. Edith Scoby

Mrs. Shari Wilson

Mrs. Anita Bonner

Ms. Juanesta Bush

Counselor

Mrs. Danita Brown

TL

Ms. Anita Harrell

DP

Dr. Jane Mosshart

Krumlauf

Ms. Alicia Nicole Lewis

Ms. Hermionne (Emmy)

Ms. Marlene Johnson

JM

Mrs. Patsy Anne

Bickerstaff

Mrs. Sonya P.

Sunshine

Woman of Worth

Marie

Mrs. Pamela Sutton

Mrs. Nicole Ellis

Mrs. Alfreada Brown-Kelly

&

All of the authors who contributed and chose to remain anonymous.